ANDERS HALLGREN ⎯⎯⎯⎯⎯⎯⎯⎯⎯⎯⎯⎯⎯

Stress, Anxiety and Aggression in Dogs

ANDERS HALLGREN

Stress, Anxiety and Aggression in Dogs

CADMOS

Copyright@ 2012 Cadmos Publishing Limited, Richmond, UK
Copyright of the original edition ©2011 by Cadmos Verlag, Schwarzenbek
Design: jb:design – Johanna Böhm, Dassendorf
Setting: Das Agenturhaus, Munich
Translation: Helen McKinnon
Editor of the original edition: Dr Gabriele Lehari
Editor of this edition: Christopher Long

Cover image: Robertino Nikolic
Photographs without credits: Dr Gabriele Lehari
Drawings: Susanne Retsch-Amschler

Printed by: Grafisches Centrum Cuno, Calbe

British Library Cataloguing in Publication Data
A catalogue record of this book is available from the British Library

Printed in Germany

ISBN 978-0-85788-204-2

Contents

Foreword

Stress, anxiety and aggression all involve almost exactly the same processes in the body, so background knowledge of this area is required urgently. Despite extensive new insights into the real causes of stress, anxiety and aggression, it is unfortunately still common practice today to treat so-called "problem" dogs in completely different ways. The most commonly used method is to suppress aggression and hyperactivity by punishing "disobedience".

Physiologically, people and dogs are very similar and their stress reactions are often identical, so there are also many examples of stress, anxiety and aggression in people. I have drawn these comparisons purely from my own experience, but we can understand our dogs' reactions much better when we are fully aware of our own.

It was the fact that many dogs are greatly distressed by the sound of fireworks that prompted me to write about stress in dogs, because I knew that something had to be done to help them. The main theme of this book is therefore anxiety and how to help dogs with psychological problems.

Many people have made important contributions to the writing of this book and I would like to express my heartfelt thanks to them. First and foremost I would like to thank psychologist David Selin, who was my student in the 1980s. He was my most helpful colleague when I was researching post-traumatic stress disorder in dogs and went on to become one of the most important lecturers on the significance of nutrition in successful therapy. I would also like to thank Lotta Arborelius, lecturer in pharmacology and stress researcher, for her valuable professional review.

Of course my thanks also go to my wife Ginger, who accepted the taciturn hours I spent in front of the computer and who was responsible for proofreading. You cannot put a high enough value on having a partner with whom you can swap ideas and who sees the text from a different point of view.

In several places the text has been simplified or generalised to make it easy to understand. This topic is being researched to such an extent that certain procedures that are considered to be successful today will not necessarily be regarded as such in the future. Explaining what stress actually means and what it causes is more important to me than presenting detailed facts.

Järna, Sweden, 2011
Anders Hallgren

Introduction

I heard the barking long before I saw the light blue VW Beetle. The German Shepherd bitch, who was just under two years old, was making such a racket in the car that the driver must have been a serious danger on the road. The owner had told me on the phone that her dog was stressed, which was something of an understatement!

The very second the dog leapt out of the car, she began running around and around in circles, like a wild thing. She had no time for sniffing, urinating or any other normal behaviour, because she could only spin around like a top. She yelped constantly as she ran because she could not go fast enough. Her owner could only get her to stop with great difficulty and when the woman leant against the car, the dog began to gallop around the vehicle.

The owner said that the dog would only relax in the house, something that the dog had probably been taught to do from the very beginning. When outside she would constantly run around in circles and it would always take her a very long time to calm down enough to take care of her basic needs.

I could sympathise with the dog because I had experienced the pressure that inner stress can cause and how it triggers stereotypical behaviour, but this compulsive behaviour did not make any sense. The dog gave up and abandoned herself to the compulsion that otherwise would have made her ill.

I got out my video camera because I wanted to show my student how an extremely stressed dog behaves.

The main reason for the stress was that the owner played lots of "fetch" games with her dog every day, which can lead to increased production of stress hormones, something that was not known at the time. Luckily, word quickly got around and such games are rare in Scandinavia today.

This is how a stressed dog can look

The dog could not work off her energy in the house, so the excess energy became bottled up and then burst out when the dog was outside.

If I had known then what I know now, we would have got much further, but as it was we progressed in small steps. After three months the dog had become considerably quieter. Although she was still very active outside, she could settle down enough to sniff and take care of a few other things.

Stress is a component of all problem behaviours and the problem cannot be solved without analysing the stress factors that play a role in the dog's life. The worst thing you can do, which unfortunately is still recommended by many trainers and used by many dog owners, is to treat the symptoms by punishing the dog for showing the wrong behaviour and praising him when he does it right.

By only tackling the symptoms you do not find out the actual cause. In the best case, this method will lead to a temporary change in the dog's behaviour, although the cause naturally still exists. A simple stress analysis tool learned

Stress can lead to total exhaustion

by students of dog psychology will immediately show the stress factors in a dog's life. And, believe me, dogs experience stress for many reasons. Often removal of the cause is enough to calm the dog and the problem behaviour will then disappear, so there is no need to find a quick fix for treating the dog. This generally involves nothing more than various types of punishment, depending on which type is currently in fashion.

Stress – a wonderful mechanism

T his chapter gives a brief overview of how the stress system works and the reasons behind it. I will give you the tools to find out whether your dog is stressed and will describe some of the typical symptoms. Many people believe wrongly that stress has something to do with illness or that it is simply damaging or harmful. However, stress actually makes a lot of sense.

Stress is present at every stage of life, at every change and in every situation. It is always there, day and night, at work and in our spare time, in our environment and also when we are alone. Stress is always present, everywhere.

It is not a flaw, an illness, something negative or something that will destroy our body and poison our soul. Stress is one of life's little miracles. It is mind and body working together.

Stress is how the body adapts to a situation

Our body's stress mechanism enables us to adapt ourselves perfectly to certain situations. Calibrated like highly accurate clockwork, the stress mechanism fine tunes our body down to the finest details. The slightest changes, even if they only take place in our head, make us tense or relaxed, depending on how we can best adapt.

If a dog looks dangerous people also become stressed

The mere thought that "I have to go to the dentist tomorrow" or "my neighbour doesn't like my dog" changes so much in me that I can feel the difference immediately. I become more alert, my heart beats faster, my breath becomes shorter and my pupils dilate slightly. Those are just some of the immediate symptoms.

This wonderful mechanism helps us when we need extra energy and greater powers of concentration, or at least when we think we do. The situations can vary greatly, for example having enough strength to lift a heavy box or needing to pass an examination at school.

The stress mechanism can also fail

The stress system can get mixed up, which happens when it is overloaded, either by a dreadful experience or when mobilisation of energy reserves is not sufficient to deal with an emergency situation.

The stress system comes into its own when we are confronted with an extreme situation, such as a serious threat or danger, or if we have to fight. Then most of the body is involved and fine tuning is no longer present. A particularly intense reaction takes place, in which body and mind respond with maximum power.

The body's own energy reserves are mobilised to counter an extreme situation. Let's say that you and your dog meet a large dog that you do not know. He looks aggressive and you know that this situation is not going to end well.

Your energy levels soar in a fraction of a second. Your strength can double and you are prepared for danger.

The brain shuts out anything that is unimportant at this moment so that you can concentrate fully on the aggressive dog and, at the same time, on protecting your own dog. There is no longer room for calculation, consideration or other thoughts. All of the brain's resources are focused on what is happening in the here and now.

The body's autonomic nervous system has reacted. This is the part of the nervous system that cannot be controlled by the conscious mind. It has, so to speak, a life of its own and enables us to adapt to everything that happens. This system consists of a network of nerves that supply the various organs.

WHAT HAPPENS NOW?

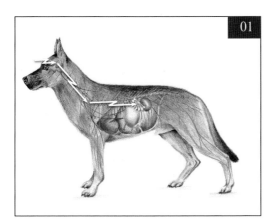

If you suddenly become frightened you feel it through your whole body as if you had been struck by lightning. That is the reaction of the autonomic nervous system. Your hair stands on end, you feel as though you are paralysed, your heart seems to stand still and you can hardly breathe (image 01).

Now the entire body, including the brain, is on red alert (image 02) and is supported by stress

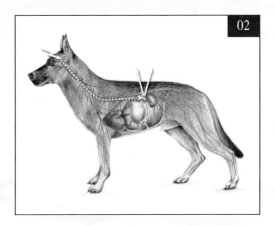

hormones, for example those formed in the adrenal cortex. When these hormones get into the bloodstream, the heart beats faster (image 03), the lungs work more efficiently, fat deposits release fat and the liver releases sugar reserves. Furthermore, blood from the stomach area and the sur-

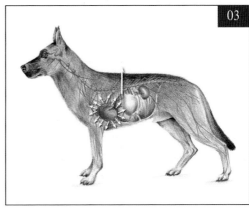

face of the skin is redirected into the muscles (image 04).

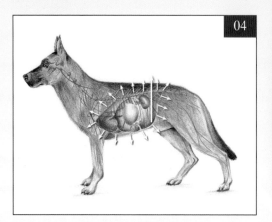

04

The stress reaction means that blood oxygen levels increase (breathing becomes more effective), and the blood is enriched with fat (fat deposits release fat into the blood) and contains more nutrients (as a result of the release of sugars by the liver). Larger quantities of blood (due to redirection of blood flow) can circulate more quickly through the body (as a result of a faster heart rate), which increases physical strength.

MORE STRENGTH

The brain is blocked by high activity. Calm, logical thought and cognition are blocked by feelings. When danger is present you do not have time to think something through calmly (image 05).

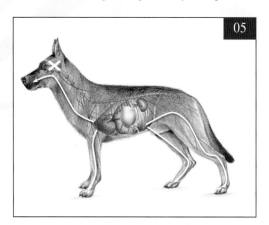

05

We all know what it feels like when anger or fear completely blocks our thoughts and renders us tongue-tied. It is only when we have calmed down that we can think about what we could have said to whoever was responsible for the stress, but by then it is usually too late.

Stress is the sign of an external or internal change that means that the individual is adapting and mobilising additional strength in order to deal with a changed situation. It could be compared with acceleration, where the body "floors it". The situation could be one in which you are exposed to a threat or danger, but it can also include a competition or a race, lifting a heavy object or many other events that require a particular strength. Energy reserves that are present in the body are used when they are really needed.

Here is an example. A man saw a car run over his young daughter. The car was not going fast, but the little girl became stuck underneath it. The man ran over, grabbed the bumper and lifted up the car, allowing others to pull the child out from underneath. Normally, the car would have been too heavy to lift. However, the stress he was exposed to made the man so much stronger that he was capable of doing something that he could not have done in a calm situation.

A stress reaction must be followed by a recovery phase

Hyperactivity can be a sign of stress

When stress becomes harmful

The faster a machine is operated, the more quickly it uses up fuel and the sooner the motor will wear out. The greater the stress and the longer it continues, the higher the risk of damage. The level of stress and the speed of wear are important when it comes to the health of a living creature. The body can withstand a lot of stress, but there are limits.

Another very important aspect is recovery or, in other words, the period of rest that is neces-sary after a powerful reaction. We need time to calm down and relax, otherwise the mind and body will become worn out.

Relaxation means not just calmness, but also recovery. The body has used up its reserves of nutrients and it takes time to build them back up again. This can take several days. Experi-encing an extreme stress reaction can be com-pared to running a marathon at high speed.

The dog's ancestors, just like our ancestors, were only exposed to dangerous and stressful situations every now and then, so they normally making derogatory comments about your dog, although stress reactions prepare us to do so.

Under closer examination, stressful situations have increased, even if most of them are not life threatening, and they occur more and more frequently in modern life. New problems arise every day, if not every hour – overwork, personal conflicts with neighbours and colleagues, fear of unemployment, money worries, time pressure, deadlines, time planning, our children's future, new diseases, family turmoil, crowds – the list is endless.

It is particularly important to investigate the circumstances that trigger stress. There is a difference between positive stress, for example an interesting new project at work, and stress caused by danger, dependence or boredom. A lot also depends on how we perceive the stressful situation: as a threat or as a challenge.

How can I tell if my dog is stressed?

In most cases, stressed dogs will be hyperactive or will overreact to certain things. The dog will often also find it hard to wait or to contain himself and will whine a little. A stressed dog will also dream more than other dogs, but because all dogs dream, it is hard to say what "more" means in each individual case.

A dog that whines a lot needs to get rid of excess energy, more energy than he is able to release at the time. Depending on what the whine sounds like, it may be a sign of stress.

If a dog has had a fright and is overcautious and easily scared then he is stressed. We can also assume that an aggressive dog that attacks other

Jumping up is often an overreaction

had time to recover in between. The amount of nutrients that the body needs to store has changed over millennia, but it was adapted originally to the lifestyle of the ancestors of modern dogs and people. Like their dogs, people today are able to cope with a certain amount of stress, but unfortunately not to the extent that is common in modern society.

Stress reactions help us to overcome difficulties using strength, but nowadays we often have to suppress our flight or fight instinct. It is not socially acceptable to beat somebody up for dogs or does not like children or certain people, for example, is under stress. A stress reaction normally occurs in order to prepare the body for fight or flight, when muscular strength is required. Stress is not necessarily the cause of the behaviour, but it can be the result, so that the dog becomes frightened or anxious easily.

However, there are other signs that point to too much stress. These are listed below in order of frequency.

Hyperactive dogs often destroy things by chewing

OVERREACTION

The reaction of these stressed dogs is exaggerated whenever something happens that attracts their attention. Instead of reacting normally in this situation, the dogs seem to blow it out of all proportion. When they meet somebody that they know, whether it is a person or a dog, they show not just happiness but full-blown exuberance. When they see a dog that they do not like they react with rage, rather than just annoyance. Such a dog does not just become frightened but is absolutely terrified in situations that are not particularly dangerous.

HYPERACTIVITY

These dogs hardly have any time to relax except at night when they are asleep or when everything is quiet in the house. They howl and chew things. When outside they are frenzied and constantly want to play. They sometimes run around for absolutely no reason at all. If they have to sit or stay somewhere, they whine or even bark. They jump up at other people and their owner and pull on the lead. They appear always to be in a hurry to be everywhere all at once. In the end it becomes too much for the owner and many of these dogs end up in rescue centres. Hyperactive dogs dream more and are livelier during their dreams than most.

IMPATIENCE

These dogs do not have the patience to wait for anything. When their owner says "let's go for a walk", such a dog immediately runs to the door and whines impatiently. If they go somewhere in the car, the dog does not lie down but whines and keeps looking out of the window. They cannot manage to stay calm.

Stressed dogs often injure their muscles because of their violent movements

If these dogs are tied up while the owner is preparing an exercise, such as an obstacle course, they howl and bark. When they get the signal to start they dart off so fast that they frequently miss part of the course out of sheer haste. If they meet a dog or a person they know when on a walk they have to greet them immediately.

"Urgent" and "immediate" are the best words to describe these dogs. They do not understand the concept of waiting patiently.

COMMON PHYSICAL SIGNS

Stressed dogs often have gastrointestinal problems, which frequently manifest themselves in the form of soft stools and a rumbling stomach. They drink, urinate and move their bowels more than other dogs. They usually like to eat large quantities of grass and sometimes they even eat twigs and lick carpets.

Stressed dogs are susceptible to infectious diseases. They also frequently suffer from muscular injuries because of their extreme, vigorous movements. They jump out of the car as soon as it stops and then run far too fast over rough terrain without warming up first.

What you should know about stress

*T*his chapter includes essential pointers to help you to understand stress reactions. Stress includes everything that an individual tries to do in order to adapt to situations in which unexpected things happen. It is like trying to keep your balance on a slippery slope so that you do not fall over. This chapter also explains how negative stress differs from positive stress.

A common misconception is that all stress is harmful. The term is sometimes equated with illness or portrayed as something negative. However, individuals can withstand a certain amount of pressure, which can even stimulate them and improve performance.

The exertion experienced when climbing a mountain, for example, can be pleasant if you decide for yourself what you are going to do and how you will do it. Having power and control over your own life is something positive. Under these circumstances you are much more involved in the activity and you feel happy and enthusiastic.

Positive stress also occurs when you are exuberant, perhaps because you and your dog have achieved something as a team at a competition or dog show.

Inner balance is important

Stress reactions are a way of restoring our inner balance. This is described as self-regulation or homeostasis. It enables an individual to function in a constantly changing environment and to be one hundred percent prepared for any situation that may arise.

Kennelling can lead to stress

Thanks to the body's ability to adjust strength, alertness and mental concentration, we can cope with difficult situations from time to time. We must always remember that we, like our dogs, are adapted to a completely different way of life from that of modern civilisation.

Mentally and physically, people and dogs are designed to live a hard life in a pitiless wilderness characterised by famine and dangerous animals. If we think about this kind of environment we can understand why stress reactions were important for our ancestors. However, nature could not have foreseen the lifestyle that people would come to share with

their dogs and the stress factors, associated with years of difficulty and problems, which unmistakably bind them.

Five important aspects of stress

Stress reactions are not the same in everyone and in all situations. Various factors determine how stress manifests itself. How great and how intense is stress for individuals? How long does it last? How do different individuals cope with stress factors in comparison to their own reactions?

Puppies should be confronted with many different environmental stimuli, in carefully measured doses

THE SUM OF ALL STRESS FACTORS

If a dog is exposed to multiple small stressful situations for a certain time, they all mount up and the dog may develop symptoms of stress. Therefore, we need to calculate the sum total of all of the stress factors.

Each of the stressful events listed below contributes to putting the dog in a predicament.

- Too many hectic games every day
- Repeated frights, for example caused by loud and unpleasant sounds
- Limited living space with several other dogs
- Too little exercise and perhaps also too little mental stimulation

This all adds up and, in total, puts a great deal of stress on a dog.

SHORT-TERM STRESS

A key word in relation to stress is "short-term". Mammals are equipped to deal with temporary difficult situations by using stress reactions.

This is what the stress mechanism is intended for. Prolonged stress becomes harmful over time, even if the stress factor itself is not very great. A constant, niggling worry over a long period of time, such as doing a stressful job every day, can lead to gastritis in people and animals.

A dog that is allowed to fetch the kill learns that a gunshot is something positive

In order to determine exactly how much stress a dog is under, it is very important that we not only add up all of the stress factors, but also that we consider how long the dog has been exposed to them.

REACTIONS DIFFER FROM INDIVIDUAL TO INDIVIDUAL

Genetic factors determine how much stress a dog can tolerate and there are considerable differences between breeds. However, there may also be differences between individuals that result from their experiences. Puppies and adult dogs who deal with stressful situations successfully seem better able to overcome problems in the future. Success makes dogs more optimistic and constructive, which is something that we recognise in ourselves.

Dogs with a healthy amount of self-confidence and the feeling that they have everything under control deal better with stress. The same applies to dogs that live an active life in a family that supports them.

STRESS REACTIONS DEPEND ON HOW THE SITUATION IS PERCEIVED

One person can experience a particular event as extremely unpleasant while somebody else

Looking away pacifies the other dog and diffuses the situation

does not find the same event to be as bad. Some people are very confident and see difficulties as more of a challenge and something that makes life a little more exciting. Others do not like to overburden themselves and wonder how other people manage to cope.

However, positive thinking can influence how you perceive a stressful situation and various types of therapy are based on changing our attitude to problems.

If a dog is frightened of gunshot and is exposed to it their nervous system is put under a lot of strain, whereas this will not affect a "gunproof" dog. Meeting strange dogs may put a dog under stress if they have learned to be cautious around unknown members of the species. For a well socialised dog with no bad experiences, this kind of encounter is positive and often leads to a game.

Dogs can reduce their negative experiences and their fear of training by associating the respective situations with fewer negative, or maybe even some positive, experiences. The hunter who lets his dog fetch the prey after the gunshot is teaching his dog that a shot is something positive. A dog that is afraid of having her claws trimmed learns to accept the procedure with positive training.

Positive stress occurs when a dog is excited about tracking work, for example

STRESSFUL EXPERIENCES DEPEND ON HOW YOU HANDLE THE SITUATION

If you find yourself in a difficult, stressful situation, for example if you are being threatened by a stranger, your experience of the situation will depend on how successfully you deal with it.

Perhaps you have the support of other people or maybe you can use diplomacy to diffuse the situation. Perhaps you will show anger, decisiveness or react with a counter threat so that the other person retreats. Stress and anxiety do not feel as bad then.

If that does not work – when there is no help from others, when diplomacy and decisiveness do not help, when you are afraid and you cannot manage the situation or get it under control – you can become very stressed and agitated.

A dog that meets another, threatening dog can look away, flatten his ears and put his tail between his legs. This ritual placates the other dog so that they can greet each other and maybe even play together.

In this case the dog has solved the problem and overcome the situation. If his behaviour had not helped and the other dog had attacked despite the pacifying signals, there would have been no option to guide the situation in another direction. In turn, this would have triggered an intense stress reaction and maybe even have led to a traumatic experience.

Some can cope with situations constructively while others prefer to avoid the issue. On the one hand it depends on the individual in question and their experiences and on the other, the degree of difficulty.

Positive and negative stress

As we have already mentioned, not all stress is negative. Inspiration, involvement and enjoyment of work can also cause stress, at least above a certain level of intensity, and this can feel good.

A tracking dog will become more alert before going out when she sees her owner getting the tracking harness, because she knows that her favourite activity is in store. A dog like this will undoubtedly get excited and whine, howl, run around and follow their owner like a shadow.

Shortly before the dog's work begins she is normally so stressed that she gets even louder and more excited. Some dogs scream, howl and bark, because they know that things are about to get started.

Despite the fact that this is a stress reaction, the dog is more happy than anything else. This is positive stress, which, if it does not get out of hand, will not put as much strain on the body as negative stress. Negative stress, however, is harmful and wearing.

Turning negative stress into positive stress is not difficult. It merely involves a suggestion – positive thinking. Using simple thought processes, negative stress can be perceived, if not as positive, then at least as neutral. For example, if you are terrified of going to the dentist you can tackle your anxiety by not thinking about the unpleasant treatment but about the good feeling that you will have afterwards.

A dog can learn that fireworks are harmless, even if he does not actually enjoy them. This can be achieved with daily training over a considerable time, using a CD or DVD of firework sounds.

Milestones in stress research

*T*here are new discoveries on the subject of stress all the time. It is therefore interesting to examine how the research began and what is behind the discovery of one of the most important topics for humans and animals.

The word stress is not old. The term was coined in the 1930s and research into stress only began around 80 years ago. Stress influences each of us, as well as all other mammals, every moment of every day, so we can see why the subject has aroused so much interest over these 80 years, and why many researchers are concerned with stress.

Stress ensures that we are perfectly adapted to every possible situation. The system concerns both small and very large, perhaps even life-threatening, events. The stress mechanism starts in the body when we meet new people, when we greet a dog, drive a car, watch an exciting film, take part in a meeting, board a crowded bus,

worry about our health, arrive late at work, argue with our nearest and dearest, get caught in a storm, are threatened by strangers (the list is endless), and continues on through all of the developments and stages of our life.

The beginning

In the early 1930s, Harvard physiology professor Walter Cannon discovered that the body tries to maintain a certain balance despite various stresses, by adapting to the environment in different ways; for example, if a situation requires us to be very strong, perhaps in order to defend ourselves against an assailant, the body can increase its muscular strength. Cannon called this "homeostasis", a kind of body self-regulation, and assumed that it was controlled by the autonomic nervous system.

Homeostasis is a key concept with regard to stress. If the organism is under extreme strain, it is like a ship in rough seas that develops a heavy list and takes on water. The whole crew have to bail out water to right the ship again. The same thing happens with mammals. When we "develop a heavy list" in life, we fight to get back on an even keel. If the situation is difficult or dangerous, muscular strength is increased to such an extent that we can come to grips with this incident and restore our balance. Later, when everything has calmed down, we also come to rest and harmonise with the current situation.

Hungarian doctor Hans Selye worked in Canada and was a fellow student of Cannon. Selye was also interested in how organisms adapt to different environmental situations and coined "stress" as the generic term for the concept. Because his English was not very good, he chose the word "stress" instead of "strain". Stress was the term that he used to describe the body's non-specific reaction to any demand or challenge in the environment. With this term, he wanted to emphasise that the body's reaction was always the same, even if the stressful situations were different.

Selye found out that this process, which he described as **general adaptation syndrome** (GAS), takes place in three stages: **alarm, resistance and exhaustion**.

- Alarm is the first stage in a stressful situation. If, for example, a large, threatening dog approaches you and your little dog, all of the body's resources are mobilised so that you are physically ready for defence or flight if the large dog attacks.

- The resistance response consists of the attempt to overcome or control the danger and tackle the threat. For example, you could take a step towards the dog and send him away while picking up your little dog. If that does not help, it may be necessary to shout for help, while fending off the big dog with your free hand. You are upset and angry when the owner of the other dog finally appears. When she then says that her dog "just wanted to play", you answer furiously that it did not look like that and that she should keep her animal under control!

- The exhaustion phase begins when it is all over. You feel limp and your knees are weak. Being upset uses up so much energy that you really have to rest in order to recover. This reflects exactly what has happened in the body. Energy reserves were used up to ward off the danger, so a period of calm is essential for building them up again. The internal organs have had to work very hard and have been weakened as a result.

If the stress continues and there is no chance to recover, the body is continually harmed and you can become ill. Such harm is caused, for example, because the heart has worked hard, the stomach has shrunk and become underperfused with blood, but has a higher acid content. The muscles have perhaps been under too much strain and the liver is working to release blood sugar. Illnesses that occur as a result decrease the immune system's performance to such an extent that it becomes compromised.

Picking up a little dog to protect it is a natural reaction when danger threatens

The physiology of stress

*I*n this chapter I deal with how the stress system works in a little more detail, although I have tried to describe it as simply as possible.

However, do not worry if you do not understand everything. Just look at it as a guide for your information that is not crucial for working with an anxious, aggressive or hyperactive dog. I will describe how to put the theory into practice later on in the book.

Stress reactions take place in three stages. The reaction of the autonomic nervous system takes place in the first stage, the second phase is the result of stress hormones and the third stage is due to the limbic system, the area of the brain responsible for feelings. All of these stages work together in a kind of symbiosis to enable the body to adapt individually to difficult situations.

We cannot control the autonomic nervous system consciously. This part of our nervous system is made up of two parts: the sympathetic nervous system, which activates the body, and the parasympathetic nervous system, which brings the body to rest.

The stress reaction

A dog is afraid of an unfriendly-looking, larger dog that is running towards her at full speed. The stress reaction starts immediately. It works like a three-stage missile. The autonomic nervous system reacts in the first stage. During the second stage, the hormones adrenaline and noradrenaline are released into the bloodstream,

Fear or aggression?

followed by the hormone cortisol 30 seconds later. Within a very short time, the dog is able to save her life by fleeing or fighting.

STAGE 1

When the sympathetic nervous system is activated, the first "command" is channelled via the nerve pathways to strengthen the heartbeat and raise the pulse. When the sympathetic nervous system reacts it feels like an electric shock in the body. The heart immediately begins to beat faster and more powerfully so that the blood can supply the body with essential nutrients faster. All of the muscles instantly become tense and the dog is ready to react to the danger in seconds.

STAGE 2

The adrenal glands are located above the kidneys, just like little caps. The autonomic nervous system activates the adrenal glands so that they release adrenaline and noradrenaline from their inner reserves, in the adrenal medulla.

These hormones are now responsible for the stress reaction in which the heart rate increases and breathing becomes faster in order to take in more oxygen, which in turn increases oxygen levels in the blood. Adrenaline is so effective that it is used in medicine to restart the heart following cardiac arrest.

The stress hormones then stimulate the liver to release additional energy from the sugar

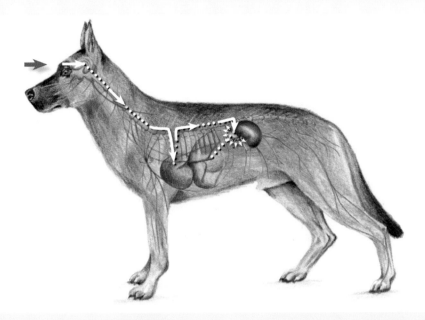

When the sympathetic nervous system is activated, the first "command" is channelled via the nerve pathways to strengthen the heartbeat and raise the pulse. The adrenal medulla then releases the neurotransmitters adrenaline and noradrenaline, which, for example, increase the oxygen and sugar content in the blood. The sugar comes from the liver. Fat is burned from the fat deposits in the body. Adrenaline also increases cardiac activity. Adrenaline is so effective that it is used in medicine to restart the heart following cardiac arrest.

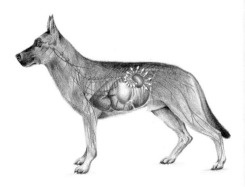

The adrenal glands are located above the kidneys, just like little caps. Adrenaline and noradrenaline are produced in the adrenal medulla, while the adrenal cortex releases cortisol.

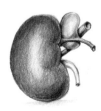

Comparison between the sympathetic and parasympathetic nervous systems

The first and fastest stress reaction takes place in the autonomic nervous system. There are two components that control a range of processes in the body – the sympathetic nervous system that activates and accelerates and the parasympathetic nervous system that limits and brakes. They exert opposite effects on the same organs.

The messenger noradrenaline is located in the nerve endings of the sympathetic nervous system. It is released when the body is exposed to stress, and physical activity helps to intensify the stress reaction. Acetylcholine is found in the nerve endings of the parasympathetic system. It has a calming and restraining effect.

The pituitary gland (hypophysis) controls the other glands in the body. The hormone released influences the adrenal cortex and therefore the release of cortisol. It is called adrenocorticotropic hormone, or ACTH.

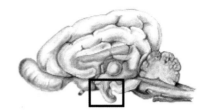

The interaction of the hypothalamus (CRH = corticotropin releasing hormone) > hypophysis (ACTH = adrenocorticotropic hormone) > adrenal cortex (cortisol) is known as the HPA axis (hypothalamus/pituitary gland/adrenal gland). This is how cortisol works during stress reactions.

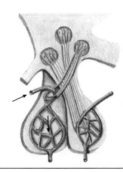

The blood transports ACTH into the adrenal cortex. The hormone is called cortisol because the outer layer is called the "cortex" in Latin.

Laughter and massage, for example, reduce cortisol levels. Sex lowers cortisol levels in women, but raises them in men. In general, women have a greater quantity of stress hormones in their blood than men. Pregnancy increases the concentration of cortisol, but so do inactivity and boredom.

reserves. The skin becomes pale as blood is diverted away from the intestines and the skin into the muscles, making the muscles larger and therefore stronger. Blood pressure rises, the pupils dilate to allow in more light, the hairs stand up to make the animal seem bigger and the blood's ability to clot improves.

The result is that large quantities of blood rich in oxygen and sugar can be transported faster through the body. Muscular strength increases significantly as a result, and sharpness of vision, readiness and activity have the highest priority.

If the sudden and unpleasant event lasts only for a short time, for example a thunderclap, a gunshot or a dog that approaches quickly but turns out to be friendly, the stress reaction fades away again. The last stage does not occur,

Adrenaline and noradrenaline force the body to direct blood from the stomach and skin into the muscles, which accelerates the heart rate and blood circulation. As a result, breathing becomes more effective and the blood is richer in oxygen. The liver also releases stored glucose. Blood pressure rises and the blood can clot more effectively. After a short time, the adrenal cortex releases cortisol, which boosts the stress reaction by releasing fat from the body's own deposits.

even though it may take a while for the dog to calm down.

After the dog has been frightened by the rapidly approaching larger dog, her eyes will appear black because of her dilated pupils. The dog's hackles will rise, she will arch her back and tail (making her appear bigger) and she will breathe heavily with her mouth open. Your dog will be ready to fight even before the bigger dog has arrived.

STAGE 3

The hypophysis or pituitary gland at the base of the diencephalon of the brain is a kind of "command gland" that controls the other glands in the body by releasing special hormones. However, the command does not flow to the relevant organs in seconds via the nerve pathways, but through the bloodstream, which takes a little longer.

If the dog sees another dog running towards her at full speed, the hypophysis channels a special hormone into the blood. This hormone influences the adrenal cortex, i.e. the outer area of the adrenal gland. The hormone is known as adrenocorticotropic hormone or ACTH. The hypophysis is thus involved in the stress reaction by stimulating the adrenal cortex to release its own hormone, cortisol.

This happens a little later, after adrenaline and noradrenaline have been released by a rapid nerve impulse. Cortisol intensifies the stress reaction, for example by causing the fat deposits to release fat into the blood, further increasing muscular strength.

The dog that sees the unknown dog running towards her has now mobilised her body in a very short time in order to increase her

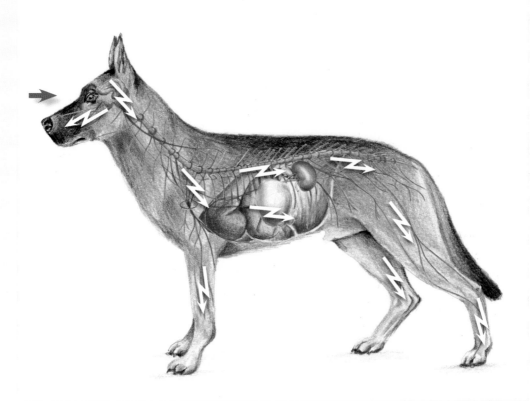

Adrenaline and noradrenaline divert blood away from the abdomen and the skin, cause sugar to be released from the liver and stimulate the heart and lungs. Cortisol reinforces the effect by releasing fat. The nutritional content in the blood increases, which boosts muscular strength. Cortisol also has an anti-inflammatory effect that helps in the event of an injury.

muscular and mental strength so that she can fight better or flee faster, depending on which strategy is best in the situation.

When the strange dog reaches your dog he stands still in uncertainty and wags his tail. He looks like a young dog that has not yet learned the right way to greet other dogs. Your dog, who is normally positive and cautious when she meets other dogs, surprises you, because she growls at the other dog and makes him back down. After a short time they start to play, although your dog is rather rough with the other one. This is probably a residual part of the stress reaction, which leads to increased muscular

Play fighting is an important part of social contact

strength, and your dog does not know her own strength at that moment.

Anger, fear and happiness

What somebody really feels is only determined to a small extent by the large amounts of hormones present. How we feel is decided primarily by the brain when it evaluates what is happening around it.

Both feelings of happiness and unpleasant events cause the concentrations of the adrenal medullary hormones, adrenaline and noradrenaline, in the blood to increase.

The adrenal cortex produces cortisol, which is described as a negative stress hormone. How-

ever, it is only negative when it is released too frequently and for too long. Increased cortisol production has a harmful affect on the immune system and makes us more susceptible to illness. For this reason, it is important that there are most rest phases than activity phases during training so that a dog can recover.

Cortisol normally has a half-life of 20 minutes (half of it will have been broken down after 20 minutes), but only under the condition that all of the stress factors have stopped. However, in today's society it is often the case that animals and people are exposed continually to stress, such as loud noises, uncertainty, monotony and high demands.

It has been demonstrated that after several days of stress the body will have cortisol levels

A gentle massage is relaxing

four times higher than normal. Some dogs that live in poor conditions are therefore constantly stressed.

Dr. Julie Lane from the Central Science Laboratory of Animal Welfare in England showed that cortisol production not only increased when work was done with remote-control electric shock collars, but the level remained high for several days, although no further training with the collars was done.

Cortisol production increases when people encounter something unpleasant, such as dangerous animals, insufferable individuals or difficult situations. Such situations can also include walking under branches full of cobwebs if you are afraid of spiders, or noticing strange shapes when walking through a graveyard at night. We often encounter crowds of people in towns and cities, for example just before Christmas when lots of people want to buy just one more gift. Crowds can also stimulate cortisol production, which leads to anxiety.

It can be unpleasant for a dog to be with other dogs that he does not like, for example when several dogs that do not get along live together in a family. If the owner is strict and unforgiving, unpleasant situations are so common that cortisol production hardly ever decreases and the dog seldom calms down and relaxes.

RECOVERY IS IMPORTANT

The so-called "flight or fight reaction" helps temporarily in difficult situations by strengthening the muscles and sharpening the senses.

If several dogs live together it is important that they get along well

However, recovery after a stressful event is essential. Stress in a specific situation is not bad, as long as it is followed by a phase of quiet and recovery. It only becomes harmful if no recovery takes place or if there is too little time for recovery. Night is normally the time for quietness and recovery, and undisturbed sleep is vitally important.

TYPE A AND TYPE B

Among people, we can differentiate between two personality types: A and B. Type A is determined and works quickly and hard, while type B is quiet and patient and works slowly and methodically. This theory about personalities is admittedly rather dated, because there are now newer descriptions such as proactive and reactive. However, I will continue to use type A and type B because they are clearer and fit better with dogs.

With type A there is a higher risk of heart attacks or ulcers than with type B, because these are the people with high adrenaline levels. They are easily frustrated and need to control everything, which means they find it hard to delegate and saddle themselves with too much

A "type A" dog

A "type B" dog

responsibility. People who like to have every-thing under control find uncontrollable situa-tions rather stressful. This trait is partly hered-itary and partly learned.

Some researchers believe that the differ-ences between type A and type B are primarily related to the male gender, at least when it comes to humans. How-ever, they all agree that there is a signifi-cant hereditary component. For exam-ple, type A rats more frequently have type A offspring, while type B rats more frequently have offspring of type B.

Don't get carried away with games of "Fetch"

TYPE A AND TYPE B DOGS

This theory can be applied to dogs very easily, although the characteristics can be assigned to breeds as well as to individuals. Sheepdog breeds are type A, whereas big, heavy dogs such as Newfoundlands or St Bernards belong to type B. Greater or lesser differences can also be found within a breed, for example if working and showing lines are bred, such as in Labrador retrievers. There are also clear individual differences between dogs with high adrenaline levels and quieter characters, regardless of breed, gender or age.

If we look at it this way, it seems logical to handle neurotic dogs more quietly, for example by avoiding too many fighting games or other things that could stress them. If the dog enjoys playing with balls or sticks, do not throw them so often that the dog becomes very wound up. Hide them so that the dog has to look for them. This not only reduces stress but mentally challenges the dog, which is just as much fun for her as it is hard work. She can still fetch the ball every now and then, but not too often.

There is no doubt that there are gender differences in adrenaline production. This may be due to the male sex hormone testosterone. In human beings it has been proven that men have higher adrenaline levels than women during peak performance, and they then achieve more than they do under lower adrenaline production. Men's reactions are determined by adrenaline. It makes them active and extrovert.

You can often tell dogs (right) and bitches (left) apart by their outward appearance alone

Other hormones associated with stress

Many other hormones play a role in stress reactions, not just the adrenal gland hormones. The adrenal glands are the most interesting and play the leading role. However, all hormones are part of a system in which everything is linked together. Sex hormones and thyroxine from the thyroid also play a role when stress occurs.

TESTOSTERONE,
THE MALE SEX HORMONE

Male dogs of most breeds are now more masculine, both in appearance and in behaviour, than they were one or two decades ago. According to

Even though the role played by testosterone has not yet been explained precisely, many investigations are currently underway and we hope that, in the future, more information will come to light about the relationship between this hormone and stress. For example, a recent discovery indicates that extreme stress in a pregnant bitch is associated with the birth of male puppies.

Frequent territory marking is extremely important for very active males

vets, dog psychologists and trainers this can be seen in countries other than just Sweden.

This is because of the criteria by which dogs are judged in the show ring. Breeders try to come up with what the judges want and, for some time now, the more masculine dogs have been in the ribbons.

Many dog owners have a hard time with their dogs. Nowadays, more and more male dogs are being castrated because of aggression towards other male dogs and other masculine behaviour. Many are euthanised or given away because they are too active and difficult to train. Sexual interest awakens far too early in these dogs and they become disproportionately interested in sex.

THE MALE SEX HORMONE HAS MANY CHARACTERISTICS

Testosterone affects male dogs in four areas: appearance, sexuality, readiness to fight, and activity.

- Male dogs are usually larger, more muscular and stronger than bitches, and they look more "manly". This is probably the main reason why dogs with a more masculine appearance do better in shows.
- Male dogs are more sexually aroused and when on walks they will constantly sniff for urine marks, which they will then urinate on. Bitches tend to be sexual objects for them, rather than playmates, regardless of where they are in their cycle.

The Labrador retriever is one of the breeds that seldom lose their appetite

- Male dogs may show aggression towards other males because testosterone increases rivalry over females. Aggression towards other males is common and is now the main reason for castration and for seeking professional help from a dog psychologist or trainer.
- Testosterone also acts like a stress hormone and makes male dogs more active, sometimes to the point of hyperactivity. The chemical effect of testosterone is similar to that of the stress hormone cortisol.

BREED DIFFERENCES

The characteristics that are the most pronounced depend on the breed and sometimes on the individual. Unless the dog is from a fighting breed, increased activity will be expressed by a greater interest in hunting, playing or procreation. In fighting breeds, levels of aggression will increase.

The appetite for food will be relatively low in entire male dogs of most breeds. Dogs will have little interest in food and are difficult to motivate with treats when training. The exceptions to this rule are ever-hungry breeds such as retrievers or spaniels that will eat under any circumstances.

CASTRATION AS AN ALTERNATIVE?

We often wonder whether it would be easier to castrate male dogs in order to avoid all of the

Thyroid problems are common in Golden retrievers

problems caused by sex hormones. There is no simple answer. There is the moral question of whether it is necessary to operate on male dogs just because we would like them to be different. It should be the breeders' responsibility to produce dogs that can fit into families and into our society.

It has also been shown that castration does not always have the desired effect. Castration is sensible if the problem concerns purely sexual behaviour, such as mounting people or other dogs, or if the male dog is only attracted to bitches on heat. When it comes to problems of aggression, castration only helps in around 50 percent of cases.

Because around 10 percent of testosterone is produced in the adrenal glands, castration only removes 90 percent, or the amount that is formed in the testicles. The remaining 10 percent can have a considerable effect if the area of the brain which is sensitive to testosterone is large, and this can vary from animal to animal. That means that the desired effect of castration is only very slight in some dogs. There is even a theory that production of testosterone in the adrenal glands increases when the testicles are removed, as well as various hypotheses that are concerned with the amount of influence that testosterone has on the brain.

Apart from the above, a castrated male may become anxious and insecure, and can sometimes also be treated badly by bitches because they think that he is another female. Furthermore, appetite can sometimes increase so dramatically after castration that their dog's constant hunger becomes a problem for the owner. The risk of thyroid problems also increases with age in these dogs.

TRY BEFORE YOU BUY

In order to minimise the risk of the unwanted side-effects of castration, vets can prescribe dogs a progesterone preparation first. Progesterone is a pregnancy hormone that counteracts the effect of testosterone – a chemical castration, so to speak. You will be able to tell what kind of effect castration would have after one or two months. Progesterone tablets are better than an injection because the effect of an injection lasts for a relatively long time and cannot be stopped if the dog has an adverse reaction to it, which is entirely possible.

Dogs should not be treated with progesterone for too long because it increases the risk of tumours.

Another alternative is the use of a chip under the skin containing a substance that regulates the influence of the pituitary gland on the testicles, so that less testosterone is released. Experiments with this method have achieved positive results. It acts like castration but can be reversed at any time. There are also various herbal remedies:

• There are many herbs that contain tiny quantities of phytoestrogens. Such herbs include various lentils and shoots such as alfalfa and hops.

• Liquorice root contains a substance that counteracts testosterone. However, liquorice must be used with caution and under veterinary supervision because it raises the blood pressure.
• St John's wort is often used as a tranquilliser and anti-depressant, but it also counteracts testosterone. A side-effect, in dogs at least, is therefore a reduced sex drive.

The simplest method for dog and owner may be to add herbs containing oestrogen to dog food. This may spare the dog tablets or an operation, and the owner a vet bill. Admittedly the effect is usually weak, but it can be surprisingly good in some dogs. However, it is important to mention that herbs can have side-effects just like medication, especially at high dosages.

THYROXINE

Thyroxine is produced by the thyroid and is involved in metabolism in different ways, but it can also influence behaviour. The following is based on an article by Norwegian vet Rita Kylling.

Overactive and underactive thyroid

If too much thyroxine is produced, we talk about hyperfunction; if too little is produced we call it hypofunction. The latter is more common in dogs, with female dogs being affected more commonly. There are two main reasons for an underactive thyroid in dogs:

1. Primary hypofunction is the most common type. It is caused by an abnormality in the thyroid, which leads to reduced capacity. The cause may be a faulty immune system reaction, whereby the cells that produce

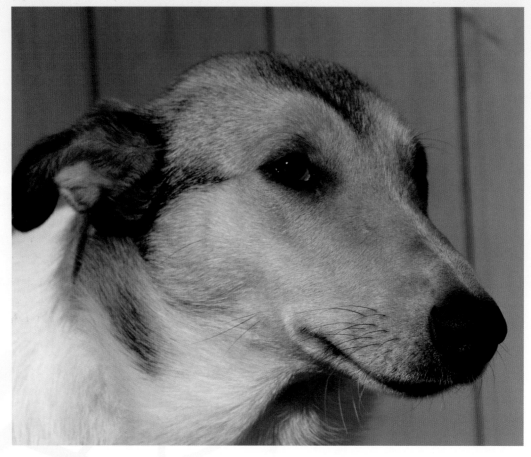

Shyness and passivity can be signs of an underactive thyroid

thyroxine are destroyed. It affects some breeds more commonly than others. The glandular tissue that produces thyroxine can also be destroyed for unknown reasons. This is known as idiopathic hypofunction.

2. Secondary hypofunction is caused by problems in the hypophysis that lead to reduced production of the TSH (thyroid-stimulating hormone). It is rare in dogs.

Thyroid problems occur mainly in middle aged and elderly dogs of certain breeds. The risk is higher in neutered dogs, both male and female.

The most common symptoms

The symptoms are vague and do not always fit together. A dog can therefore suffer from an underactive thyroid without their owner knowing. The owner just thinks that their dog's behaviour is slightly different from normal. Hypofunction may cause the following signs:

- Weakness and passivity
- Tendency to gain weight easily
- Reluctant to do physical exercise, tires quickly
- Low tolerance of cold temperatures, gets cold quickly, seeks heat
- Skin problems (present in around 60 percent of cases): dry skin, scurf, quality and colour of coat change, hair loss, stronger coat colour, thickened skin, itching, skin infections, poor wound healing
- Reproductive cycle changes, miscarriage, small litters with low birth weight puppies, weak puppies, stillbirths
- Mental retardation
- Low body temperature
- Rapid pulse
- Behaviour problems such as timidity and aggression

Thyroid hormone production can sometimes be influenced by treatment with various medications (such as corticosteroids and antibiotics), certain illnesses (such as diabetes), liver and kidney problems, general strain, heat, pregnancy and phantom pregnancy, and age (thyroxine production is high until the 12th week of life and only then does it stabilise at a lower level). Daily fluctuations are normal. There are also differences among breeds. For example, greyhounds and deerhounds usually have a lower level of thyroxine than other breeds. If you suspect that something is not right with your dog's thyroid, your vet should perform a blood test. Even though the risk of disease is low, a blood test can still be sensible, especially if you are having a lot of problems with your dog.

The brain – how it functions under stress

The brain controls the body, even under stress. The brain is supposed to keep everything in balance so that we react, but do not overreact, to allow us to adapt continually, within seconds, to changes in our environment. The brain helps us to raise stress to an optimum level and to calm down when it is essential. Without this extremely important control we would "burn out" in no time.

The structure of the brain

There are differences between humans and dogs when it comes to brain size. The brain of an average-sized dog weighs around 130 grams, a chimpanzee brain weighs around 400 grams and a human brain weighs 1500 grams. Apart from weight, one of the major differences is that the neocortex of the human brain is larger and better developed than in other mammals.

The neocortex has various functions, including sorting, organising and coordinating

The neocortex is the outer layer that best demonstrates the differences among different animal species. Its grooves and folds make its surface area very large. In human beings, the neocortex comprises around 15 billion active nerve cells, compared with just a few billion in dogs.

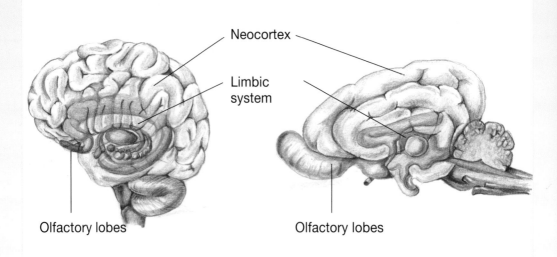

Neocortex

Limbic system

Olfactory lobes

Olfactory lobes

Comparison between human and canine brains

In mammals, the limbic system is surrounded by a "newer" layer, the neocortex. In humans, the newer mammalian brain is the command centre for thought processes and language. The more highly developed a mammal is with regard to cognition, the larger the neocortex in comparison with the limbic system.

A major difference between people and dogs is that the olfactory lobes, the part of the brain that processes olfactory information, are larger in dogs, which is one reason for dogs' excellent sense of smell.

Dogs live in a world full of smells that define their emotions just as much as visual and auditory stimuli influence our feelings, or perhaps even more. For example, think about what you feel when you hear the song "White Christmas". In dogs, there is a direct link between the sense of smell and the state of mind.

Excessive panting can be a sign of stress

information from our senses. Many cognitive processes, such as logical thinking, take place in the frontal lobes in particular, and injuries to the forehead can have a negative effect on cognitive function.

The area that is primarily concerned with emotions is located deeper in the brain. It is called the limbic system and branches out to the cerebral cortex.

Homeostasis – balance in the different levels of the brain

In the last chapter we looked at the importance of homeostasis, or self-regulation, where the organism endeavours to maintain balance in various situations. For example, if the body overheats it is cooled down by evaporation – humans sweat and dogs pant. If the body needs nutrients you feel hungry or lightheaded and need to eat something urgently. The body behaves in the same way with stress reactions, whose aim is to make sure that balance is maintained in relation to the environment. When something is urgent, such as a threat, a balance has to be created in order to be able to deal with this situation.

The brain normally plays a leading role in these processes. Above all, it needs to find the right balance between activity and calm, in order to activate or restrain the organism.

This balance influences stress reactions to such an extent that if we feel very hurt, we become blocked and may react emotionally. At other times the reaction is hindered and restricted and we calm down and can think clearly again. We talk about "accelerating" and "braking", and in these processes very different regions of the brain are involved in numerous ways.

Balancing of reactions seems to be so important that there is not just one but various systems in the brain that work in conflicting ways. It is like the control and balance that we see in a set of scales, where one weight balances out the other.

One area accelerates when necessary; another brakes if required. This system exists on various levels, with regard to both the areas of the brain and various neurotransmitters. That is why it is so important that the control systems work together.

This is a rather simplified explanation. In reality, the processes are much more complicated, but I have presented it in shortened form to make it easier to understand.

THE SYMPATHETIC NERVOUS SYSTEM AND THE PARASYMPATHETIC NERVOUS SYSTEM

As mentioned above, the autonomic nervous system is not controlled consciously. It is divided into two areas: sympathetic and parasympathetic. The autonomic nervous system controls functions such as sweating, glands and their secretions, cardiac activity, blood pressure, breathing and so on. When you are stressed, the sympathetic nervous system activates various organs, while the parasympathetic nervous system has an opposite or inhibiting effect on these same organs. For example, the sympathetic nervous system raises the heart rate, while the parasympathetic nervous system slows it down.

Thus, these two areas work against each one another – one accelerates; the other brakes. That way they ensure balanced stability in every situation so that there should not be too much or too little activity.

If a situation requires a quick reaction, for example if you are being threatened, activity is increased. When the situation returns to normal, the sympathetic nervous system should be less active and the parasympathetic nervous system should come into action to create a balance so that the internal organs do not tire prematurely.

THE TWO HALVES OF THE BRAIN

The left and right halves of the brain process information in different ways. The right controls the emotions (sadness, fear, anxiety, happiness) and the left is responsible for logical and cognitive areas (evaluation, consideration, calculation). The left half is the "analyst"; the right is the "creative". Naturally, however, the two

Stroking calms the dog and strengthens the bond with its owner

areas are not completely separate and functions overlap between the two halves of the brain.

We have been able to establish that thoughts are slow and emotions are fast. This means that the left half of the brain, which is responsible mainly for cognitive, slow processes, can slow down the faster, emotional processes in the right half.

THE LIMBIC SYSTEM AND THE FRONTAL LOBES

The limbic system is located in the deeper, older area of the brain. Emotions are mainly processed in the limbic system, which has many nerve pathways that lead to other areas of the brain.

The most important role of the limbic system is to regulate feelings and instinctive behaviour, as well as essential biological functions.

Most feelings seem to originate in this region. The lower part of the limbic system receives impulses from the amygdala. These stimuli are mainly related to aggression, fear and sexual behaviour. Feelings such as anger, fear, worry, euphoria and sexual interest can be caused by electrical stimulation of the amygdala. Electrical stimulation of the amygdala can cause fear even when no threat is present.

A dog can only concentrate when it is calm

Unlike the limbic system, the cerebral cortex controls rational thought. The frontal lobes are involved mainly in cognitive, logical thinking. However, because of the links between the limbic system and the cortex, emotions can be influenced by logic and vice versa. When you are calm, thoughts are simple, logical and clear. That is when the cortex and the frontal lobes are active. If you become nervous, anxious or angry, rational processes are blocked by the active limbic system. If you are angry, afraid or upset you can calm down by talking to yourself

or somebody else because these strong feelings are blocked by the activity of the cortex that is involved in speaking.

It does not take much activity in the feelings centre, the limbic system, before cognitive processes are inhibited in the neocortex, i.e. thinking is blocked. This happens frequently to all of us and we can see it in other human beings. They become upset and are suddenly rendered speechless, or may even scream, when it is too difficult for them to talk about a problem logically and calmly. It is virtually impossible to solve a mathematical problem or to make plans for the future when you are miserable or crying.

A dog cannot concentrate on solving a task or learning something if she is upset for any reason, even just an unknown dog coming too close.

Conversely, it is the same when you are concentrating on a logical task and have to think rationally. Feelings are blocked. You cannot laugh or cry at the same time as being occupied with constructive thought processes or with solving a problem logically.

A dog that is concentrating fully on something, such as following a trail, does not become stressed, even if there are other dogs close by. Another example is a cat engrossed in watching a mouse hole. The cat appears to be deaf and blind to anything that is happening around him.

This is another system that ensures that there is a balance between spontaneous emotions and considered thought processes at any given

moment. Sometimes, you will stop perceiving anything around you and react at lightning speed, perhaps because you fear for your life. On another occasion you will be calm, logical and focused enough to solve a task. That happens to dogs too.

THE LINK BETWEEN NORADRENALINE AND SEROTONIN

Chemical messengers convey electrical nerve impulses to various substations in the body. They work most effectively when cognitive and emotional reactions are balanced.

A nerve pathway has many relay stations that forward nerve impulses. These relay stations are the synapses (see illustration), which are gaps that contain the fluid required for forwarding the impulses.

Noradrenaline is produced by the adrenal glands only in small quantities. This hormone is a messenger that conveys nerve impulses. It is primarily formed in the nerve endings and plays

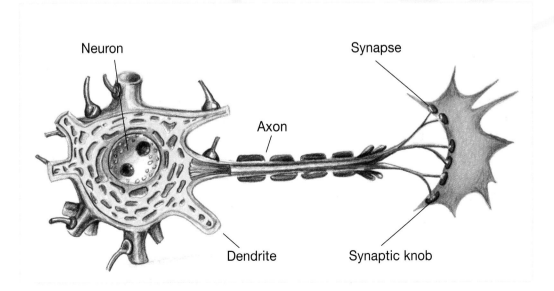

Neuron

Synapse

Axon

Dendrite

Synaptic knob

This dog is clearly expressing stress and anxiety

Synapses and nerve impulses

Some nerve cells contain noradrenaline, which stimulates brain activity. Other nerve cells contain serotonin, which inhibits or slows down brain activity.

a most important role in the synapses between nerves, where it transmits the nerve impulses.

Certain nerve cells are activated by the "accelerator" noradrenaline, which increases activity. These nerve cells are distributed throughout the entire body, in all of the nerve pathways of the sympathetic nervous system, not just in the brain. When they are stimulated the speed and intensity of activity in the muscles increases.

Other nerve cells in the brain are controlled by serotonin, which reduces anger, fear and tension. This calms the brain so that it does not get out of control and balances out reactions.

Noradrenaline and serotonin work against each other in order to create the balance required for an optimum reaction in different situations. After a very stressful phase or after one or more traumatic experiences (particularly after a shock at a young age) there is thought to be an imbalance in the interaction between noradrenaline and serotonin. Activity in the noradrenaline cells will then be dominant, while too little happens in the cells that are influenced by serotonin.

The symptoms are obvious. We tense up, become sensitive to sound and jump at unexpected noises or anything that happens suddenly, we are nervous, dream more than normal, are often anxious or aggressive, always on the alert and demonstrate behaviour patterns that are described as nervous.

THE AMYGDALA AND HIPPOCAMPUS
The limbic system is the location of the amygdala, a tiny structure shaped like an almond. It

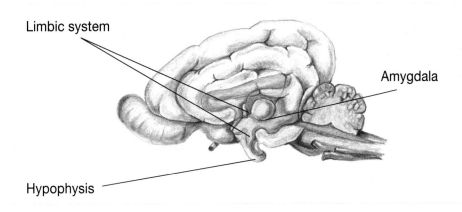

Limbic system

Amygdala

Hypophysis

The amygdala stimulates cortisol production as part of the stress system – the system is known as the HPA axis (hypothalamus/pituitary gland/adrenal gland).

is the centre for powerful emotions such as aggression and fear. Close by is another small centre, the hippocampus, which counteracts the amygdala, as well as other systems. The hippocampus is active on a cognitive level; it calms and analyses and reduces the effect of the emotions stimulated by the amygdala.

Furthermore, there are many chemical messengers that are able to trigger different sensations such as harmony, happiness and joy (oxytocin), calmness and pain relief (endorphins), and so on.

The hippocampus constantly compares sensory stimuli with a learned pattern of expectation. As long as the environment does not change, or as long as the changes are expected, the hippocampus remains active and suppresses emotions so that we can use the neocortex and the frontal lobes for reason, creativity and logical thought. Patients with minor injuries in the hippocampus area have problems with concentration and alertness. Their thoughts, experiences and memories are disrupted by insignificant changes in the environment.

Accelerating	Braking
Sympathetic nervous system	Parasympathetic nervous system
Left half of the brain	Right half of the brain
Limbic system	Neocortex/frontal lobes
Noradrenaline	Serotonin
Amygdala	Hippocampus

Some dogs have difficulty controlling their reactions and become frantic

Shaped like a seahorse (hippocampus is the Latin word for seahorse), the hippocampus can reduce stress and create relaxation.

Impulsivity and control

Some dogs seem to find it hard to control or restrain their reactions. They are temperamental and have a bold and engaging personality. When you say "let's go!", these dogs are the first to the door. They whine, cannot stand still and jump up and down. They are in a tearing hurry and rush outside as soon as the door opens. They whine almost constantly in the car, as if they cannot control themselves, until they arrive, regardless of the destination. When they want to greet a person or a dog that they know, they pull on the lead and can hardly wait until they get to their friend. When they are annoyed they become upset and overreact, and if they are frightened, they often react with panic.

These are examples of inadequate impulse control, which apparently correlates with insufficient serotonin activity in the brain. Of course, these same symptoms can also be caused by other types of stress and by over- and understimulation.

A "show" Labrador

A "working" Labrador

A dog with insufficient impulse control can also react to pain, in particular, because pain upsets him, but also because he quickly becomes stressed or "acts mad". A dog that is in pain will quickly learn that it hurts less when he is under stress.

We suspect that stress causes more endorphins to be released and endorphins relieve pain. They are known as the body's own morphine. Of course, people react in the same way – the calmer you are the more pain you feel.

Moderate stress caused by pleasant experiences can mean that we feel less pain. Laughter therapy, where patients get together to tell jokes, can soothe pain for up to an hour.

It has been established that the noradrenaline and serotonin systems are hereditary to a large extent. To a certain degree, this could explain the differences between breeds, or between bloodlines within the same breed of dog (such as working and showing lines). We do not yet know what the underlying genetic process is, but investigations in the future will provide the answers. A diet balanced in nutrient content probably also plays a major role.

However, it is important to clarify the cause of a lack of control in a particular dog. We must not jump to the conclusion that it is necessarily caused by an imbalance in the messengers in the brain.

Stress creates imbalance

The stress system primarily influences the relationship between emotions and logical thought. It is extremely important that we are always in equilibrium with our environment. If something unexpected happens, we use our feelings because they can deal with new situations quickly. At that moment, all cognitive functions are switched off because they work too slowly. When everything has calmed down, we switch back to logical thinking and our emotional reaction subsides.

The words "stable" and "unstable" are used commonly. A stable person can adapt quickly to any changes and react to them well. A stable dog is flexible and adapts easily to events without overreacting. This kind of dog is happy when she is fed or when she goes for a walk, but does not run around excessively, whine, pant or have problems calming down.

An unbalanced person reacts with bewilderment, desperation, anger or even fear when things change in their life. They will be full of worry and take a long time to get used to the change. An unstable dog cannot calm down when he has been told that it is time to go for a walk. He whines, whimpers and runs around, which makes putting on his collar and lead difficult. If he sees another dog he pulls on his lead, barks and gets very worked up.

All of the various control systems inside and outside the brain contribute to the equilibrium. Sometimes it works; sometimes it does not. Reasons for this vary from genetic makeup to life experiences.

This dog exudes balance

The balance between emotion and logical thought

One of the brain's important roles is to ensure that feelings and thoughts work well together. Feelings are responsible for fast reactions, they differ from individual to individual and they determine behaviour in the moment, whereas thoughts work more slowly and are more profound.

FAST FEELINGS

Reactions on an emotional level are necessary when we are surprised or when things happen quickly, when our "gut instinct" tells us what to do, such as during a sudden attack by a threatening person. It is a matter of reacting quickly, either by fleeing or by defending yourself. This also includes threatening situations that have been anticipated, for example if severe weather is approaching and we need to be prepared in case something happens. However, it may also be a pleasant surprise, for example if a friend that we have not seen for a long time suddenly appears at our door and we are overcome with happiness.

The same thing happens with dogs. Dogs will have many experiences like this, even on a short walk. Just think about all the different scents of other dogs, from the scent of bitches on heat to the markings of their arch enemy. They often meet other dogs on a walk, both friends and enemies. Suddenly fleeing animals or strangely dressed people (who are mysterious, perhaps threatening and out of the dog's view) may appear unexpectedly in a forest or park. A gun may go off somewhere nearby or a loose dog may suddenly appear. There is a constant need to adapt to different circumstances.

Motivation and commitment are usually governed by feelings. If you are motivated and committed, you engage yourself fully and it feels good. Solving a difficult problem can be fun: "it'll be alright in the end!" You feel as if you have had a little lottery win. "I'm on a winning streak – next time I'll hit the jackpot." A dog experiences similar feelings when she finds the "missing" object on a trail.

Emotional reactions contribute to doing good work with better results. Reactions include muscular strength, as in the case of the man whose little daughter ended up under the car. He managed to lift up the car and save his daughter. Emotional reactions enable us to act quickly. When something happens suddenly, for example if a dangerous dog appears in front of us, there is no time for reflection. You either run away or try to make the dog run away. You do not have time to choose logically between the two alternatives. Instead, you have to act, no matter what happens.

EMOTIONS BLOCK THOUGHTS

When something happens that requires us to act, emotions come into play. The sympathetic nervous system starts up as if we had flicked a switch.

The limbic system reacts and sends nerve impulses into other areas of the brain. The more urgent, important, dangerous or pleasant something is, the more powerful the reaction.

The adrenal gland produces the stress hormones adrenaline, noradrenaline and cortisol, which leads to stress reactions appropriate to the situation.

Such a situation could be a competition for which I have been preparing my dog for months. Perhaps my work with the dog welfare society, where I explain to school children the effect that fireworks can have on dogs, is also involved. Perhaps it is a visit to the vet, where I am nervously awaiting my dog's test results, so I can find out if he has a serious illness. It can also be the exuberance of my dog when he meets his best friend and his happiness transfers to me.

In all of these situations, as well as other situations that trigger strong feelings, there is no time to reflect or consider, because thoughts are blocked by emotions. How often does somebody say something mean or stupid that makes you feel inferior and upset? Words fail you so you cannot come up with a retort. Later, when your heart is no longer beating so fast and you have calmed down a little, you think of every possible response. Now you know exactly what you should have said, if you had just been quick enough. But yes, it's a bit late now...!

Everybody will undoubtedly have seen how a dog can suddenly become blocked, how she appears to have become deaf, despite the person raising their voice. This is not intentional defiance, but a case of the emotions blocking the brain.

Creeping up with a crouched posture is one of a dog's greeting rituals

SLOW THOUGHTS

Thought processes, such as serious reflection and consideration, are slow. They require more cognitive input than feelings do. First all of the pros and cons need to be balanced out, different strategies need to be developed, and consequences need to be considered. This delays our reactions, but concentration can block feelings in the same way that emotions can block thoughts. These things apply to our dogs to a similar extent.

If we are confronted suddenly with a threatening or dangerous situation, considerations and healthy human intellect must not stand in the way otherwise we risk harm because we may react too slowly. If a bad guy approaches us brandishing a baseball bat, it does not make any sense to mull it over. "Hmm, he wants to attack me. Which strategy would be the best? Should I …? Or perhaps …?" Valuable seconds would tick by and the opportunity for flight or to prepare for defence would have been missed.

If a dog sees a loose dog running towards him, there is no time to think about whether he wants to play or attack and there is no time to decipher the body language of the approaching dog.

That is certainly one of the reasons why dogs have such clear signals for their greeting rituals. A dog will not usually run up to another dog too quickly, but if she does she gives clear signals, by crouching down or acting as if she is going to run past. If she runs up to another dog recklessly without clearly signalling her peaceful intentions, the consequences can be fatal.

CONTEMPLATION IS IMPORTANT – SOMETIMES

Thoughts and feelings can block each other out. In some situations, it is very important and correct that we react emotionally, quickly and with commitment, but sometimes it is better to act sensitively and logically. It is best to find a balance, an intermediate path between thinking and feeling, adapting and conforming, depending on the situation.

DRIVING

Our reactions when we are driving a car are a wonderful example of how thoughts and feelings influence us. When we are calm, we are attentive and measured at the wheel and we concentrate on what we are doing. We drive with foresight, using our frontal lobes. We show consideration and respect to other road users, letting drivers merge, braking in time for junctions and actually stopping at stop signs. Other motorists behind us may wonder at our accurate and unhurried style of driving.

When we are in a hurry or wound up, perhaps after an argument, our driving is fast, aggressive and lacks consideration. We are now driving with our limbic system. We become bolder and bolder, taking risks, shoving in front of other cars and not letting anybody into our lane if there is a chance they could get in our way. Our car comes screeching to a halt at junctions and we drive through stop signs. We overtake the crawling "Sunday drivers" (who drive like we do when we are not controlled by our emotions) at high speed and brake in front of them, so that they are in no doubt that they are driving too slowly. We want to show others the right way to drive.

We can compare the social behaviour of dogs with a team sport

Think about it – all of that can happen within the same person, but at different times.

TEAM SPORTS

Team sport is a revealing example of the importance of balance and flexibility between sensitivity and emotions and, above all, team sports resemble the behaviour of wild canids when they cooperate on hunts.

We can observe fast and emotional or slow and tactical moves in ice hockey. The fast game is based mainly on speed. The players act emotionally and use the area of their brain that is associated with fast, emotional processes – the limbic system and the right half of the brain. This leads to the fewest passes possible between players, although it results in a lot of recklessness, collisions and unfair play. The players are in such a hurry that they forget that they are playing in a team and are more worried about being fast and taking risks.

On the other hand there are players that play according to plan and follow a strategy, slowly and purposefully. They think during

When puppies play together they take turns at being hunter and prey

the game, so their opponents can snatch the puck from them. Their strategy determines how the puck is passed and how attack and defence play, in which areas of the pitch and at which point. If they stick to the agreed tactics, they have to use the cognitive, slower areas of the brain – the frontal lobes of the neocortex – to concentrate on the game.

And then there are ice hockey teams that rehearse strategies slowly and precisely first so that they can gradually increase their tempo, while the strategies remain in place. The Soviet team used this kind of training to win the most caps in the 1970s. They managed to achieve an effective balance between the areas of the brain that use logical thinking and those that produce emotions.

A HUNTING PACK

A wolf pack acts like a successful team. A pack uses both inherent and learned strategies when hunting. The animals have practised this team-work many times, starting from a young age. To begin with they learn through play and, later on, they refine the game with real hunts. In reality the prey often gets away, which forces the pack to work together better and to refine their strategy. The wolves do not all attack the same part of the prey, but seize different parts of the victim's body from different directions.

The pack members have learned to observe each other and can probably perceive the others' signals almost continually and communicate with each other, although they are concentrating on the prey.

They have learned:

- How to position themselves in relation to the others and with regard to the prey
- When to attack and when to retreat
- Where they should attack and what they should avoid (such as hooves or horns)
- When to divert the prey
- When the prey has been bitten, i.e. held, enough to injure it

Wolves are like a successful ice hockey team. They can perfectly balance the cognitive and emotional areas of the brain.

Stress and personality

Each individual reacts differently to stress, which also depends on a variety of factors. While one dog (or person) will be upset and despondent when something unpleasant happens, the same event will not make any difference to somebody else. Countless factors determine how sensitively people react to stress. It is not possible to describe all of these factors, but the main ones that affect dogs are given below.

The basis for how sensitively or robustly a dog deals with stress is a combination of genetic disposition and environmental factors. Above all, early stress caused by certain events or training methods and traumatic events in the early years are critical here. Even changes in the balance of various chemical substances play a role, such as a poor supply of nutrients or the inability to use certain nutrients for the construction of chemical messengers. One example of this is the inability to absorb certain B vitamins.

This can influence the development of a dog's personality, at least with regard to temperament. Is he quiet or nervous, anxious or brave, bold or cautious, cheerful or serious, playful or lazy, confident or unsure? All of this is mainly decided by the brain, as a sum of its experiences and chemical processes.

Chemistry and personality

One theory that researchers have developed about personality is of particular interest here.

Serotonin is made from the amino acid tryptophan. Dopamine and noradrenaline are derived from the amino acid tyrosine. Tryptophan and tyrosine compete to penetrate nerve cells, during which tyrosine "eats" '(chemically digests) tryptophan.

The attraction of this hypothesis is that it links certain personality traits to some of the best known messengers, namely serotonin, noradrenaline and dopamine.

Cereals contain a lot of tyrosine, which means that you may have to be careful when feeding them in large quantities – check the ingredients of your dog food. However, if your dog does not show any signs of stress and enjoys her food then you do not need to worry about whether the food contains cereals.

It is important that you know how the various chemical messengers and their antagonists interact. They exert an influence on each other and are in turn influenced by a series of apparently insignificant circumstances.

Stress factors in dogs

*V*arious stress factors are encountered by people and dogs, on the one hand because of biological programming handed down by their various antecedents and, on the other, because life today is perceived differently.
In this chapter, I will describe in detail the factors that influence a dog's tolerance of stress, the most common stress factors that we impose on our dogs, and something that occurs all too frequently – trauma.

Anything and everything in our environment, as well as our "inner core", including feelings, can influence our inner activity to a lesser or greater extent. The more powerful the effect, the greater the inner activity. Our stress mechanism reacts in very different ways, so that we are prepared for whatever happens – from sleep and relaxation to a panic attack. Everything that triggers a stress reaction is described as a stress factor.

Hereditary characteristics

Genes are also partly responsible for stress, although it is hard to say exactly what role they play.

This becomes obvious particularly when we compare different breeds with one another. Some are quiet, balanced and stable, while others are easily stressed, temperamental and apparently uncontrollable.

The character of the bitch will often determine whether or not her offspring are quiet

Prenatal stress

Components of the blood of a pregnant bitch flow through her puppies' veins when they are still foetuses, and many hormones are transported in this way. It has been found that pregnant dogs who are exposed to high levels of stress give birth to puppies that tend towards stress when they grow up. The same has been found in people. Mothers that undergo traumatic experiences have children who are susceptible to problems with stress.

The calming effect of gently stroking the belly of a pregnant bitch is transferred to the puppies in her womb and helps them to relax. In turn, this can bring about an emotional connection between the puppies and their mother, and even have a positive effect on the socialisation process.

Early influences

Everybody is extremely sensitive and "programmable" when their life begins. Early experiences that increase or reduce sensitivity to stress in any way may have a lifelong impact. If, for example, a puppy is exposed to cold for a long time, he will probably have a greater tendency to stress, because the increased nor-

Early handling makes puppies stronger and more resilient

adrenaline activity influences other stress systems.

Tolerance to stress will increase if the puppy is cared for, picked up and given a little cuddle every day. The more he is stroked, to a certain extent, the greater the effect. This is described as "handling".

As proof of this theory, American researcher Michael Fox exposed puppies to daily systematic handling during the first weeks of their life. They were lifted up, carried around, placed on a rotating table like a slow carousel, weighed, turned on their backs and so on. Each session did not last for very long, but led to impressive results. When they grew up, these dogs were astonishingly tolerant of stress and could endure situations that made other dogs extremely upset.

One possible explanation is that handling triggered mild stress and led to increased noradrenaline activity, to which the brain responded by increasing serotonin activity. The puppies' inner balance system reacted to the slight stress by releasing the "braking" hormone serotonin, setting the pattern for stressful experiences in later life. The period of particular socialisation also made the puppies stronger and more resilient.

However, it is worth mentioning that too much handling can be a stress factor for young puppies. It is hard to say where exactly the boundary

Developing a bond with people as early as possible is very important

lies, and some people believe that puppies should not be exposed to any systematic handling at all.

Imprinting and bonding

Imprinting is the genetically determined process that all young animals undergo early in life. It is the phase during which they learn which species they belong to. If, for example, a newborn lamb is raised by people and does not have any contact with its mother or other sheep, it will later be afraid of sheep and will only interact with humans. The terms bonding or socialisation are sometimes used in modern behavioural research instead of the term imprinting. They are all used to describe the process that the young animal goes through.

Socialisation includes bonding with other animals of the same species, a kind of identification, and it is a component of early development. Certain authors claim that imprinting only occurs in animals that are already well developed at birth, such as hoofed animals and many birds. Virtually unlimited interaction with their parents is possible for them almost from the beginning. On the other hand, animals whose offspring are born blind and deaf have to undergo socialisation for several weeks, during which they also learn to recognise members of their own species.

Puppy classes are important for meeting lots of different dogs

Today's behavioural researchers are critical of bonding in two ways. On the one hand, they argue that young animals learn who their parents are but not which species they belong to and, on the other hand, they argue that they also get to know their siblings.

When dogs become sexually mature, their choice of partner is significant in the sense that the partner must not be too similar (such as a brother or sister), to reduce the risk of inbreeding, but also not too different. That would lead to problems, such as the reduction of their own gene pool and the inability to pass on heritable features.

A puppy recognises people and dogs by sight and hearing. But above all, she recognises the individual scent of the breeder, of her siblings and her own mother. It could therefore be said that the puppy thinks that humans and dogs belong to the same species, despite the fact that they look completely different.

One reason why puppies should never be born or raised in a puppy farm therefore becomes clear. Little contact with humans at an early stage of life can lead to great problems later on if the dogs are intended to live in human families. Moving into their new home would be like meeting aliens, without the option of communication or understanding their behaviour. The dog would feel like a creature from another planet.

Socialisation

Socialisation is crucial for a dog's development. A puppy should have plenty of opportunities to meet nice dogs and people of all ages, as early on in life as possible, because the socialisation phase comes to an end at just twelve weeks. After that it becomes much more difficult to influence the puppy's relationship to others.

A small number of people and dogs can be enough for a good socialisation, but they should all be very different. The puppy has to learn to accept people and dogs of all sizes. Think about how many different people he will meet in later life. Some will be clumsy, some will be nice, some will be angry and most will smell very different to a dog's sensitive nose. The variety is enormous.

A part of socialisation that is often overlooked is introducing puppies to adult dogs. Many puppies do not have the chance to get to know a male dog, with his special scent, because their father lives elsewhere and the breeder does not have any adult dogs. If, at the age of ten or eleven weeks or even later, a puppy is confronted for the first time with an animal that looks like a dog but that smells completely different, he may be afraid.

THE MOTHER

The age at which a puppy moves in with a human family is extremely important. According to Scott and Fuller, the age of seven or eight weeks is ideal. However, we must also bear in mind that there are differences between breeds and sometimes between individual animals in this respect.

Puppies are not able to be taken away from their mother before the seventh week, for various reasons. They are not mature enough to leave their mother, either physically or in terms of social behaviour. Evidence that the brain is not fully developed before the fifth week of age is given by the fact that an electroencephalogram (EEG) trace only shows a similar pattern to that of an adult dog from this age onwards. The brain is also flooded with enormous amounts of information during this period that it has to process so that it can react to situations, and so that it can grow and develop. Furthermore, the puppy needs the first seven or eight weeks to learn everything possible from her mother and to be with her brothers and sisters. In terms of communication alone, a puppy has to learn an entire language in no time at all.

The more time that elapses after the eighth week of life, however, the more detrimental it is. A puppy that is not given away until after its 12th week of life is at risk of developing neophobia, i.e. a fear of anything new or of situations that she has never experienced before. She will crawl under the bed or into a corner in her new home. New people, dogs and objects – everything that she is not accustomed to is dangerous in her eyes. This would not have happened if the puppy had got to know her environment earlier. Hardly a good start in life!

Environmental training is essential here. If a six- or seven-week-old puppy can get to know different places – gently and cautiously – she will become used to different environmental stimuli and the risk of neophobia will decrease substantially.

Environmental training is just as important as social training

The longer a puppy lives with her siblings, the closer they will become. Perhaps one is a bully and the other learns to avoid confrontation. In this case the development of two different personalities has already been consolidated. Again, there are also individual and breed differences here.

Unfortunately it has become more and more common to wait until ten weeks before giving puppies away. In light of the arguments given above, this is the latest possible time. However, if the breeder gets the puppy used to environmental stimuli, as well as to people and other friendly dogs, the negative effect can be reduced drastically.

SOCIAL SKILLS

Social training is also important. While puppies learn about other animals and people through socialisation, social training teaches them how to behave towards others, and which rules are important.

Puppy courses are ideal not just for training the puppy, but also for improving their social skills. It is important to learn the right way to behave, communicate and how to integrate into society.

ADAPTATION TO DIFFERENT ENVIRONMENTS

Environmental training is at least equally important. A puppy must be able to adapt to all of

Puppy classes involve a combination of playing and learning

the different environments that he is likely to encounter as part of modern life and to accept them. From the age of six or seven weeks, puppies should be confronted with a few different environmental stimuli at once, without being put at risk. This sometimes happens automatically when the breeder takes the puppies to the vet for a check-up or gets them used to a new environment in the neighbourhood. However, that is not enough if the puppies are not going to be given away for a long time.

Puppies that grow up with very few stimuli, and those that are excluded and unable to gain enough experience, have the greatest problems in the future. This can happen on large breeding farms where puppies live in big kennels, but also when puppies grow up in houses but are kept in the cellar or other restricted areas and do not have enough contact with the rest of the household.

Diet

Another possible stress factor is food and its ingredients. Dietary deficiency can cause stress if the food is inadequate or unbalanced, or does not meet the needs of a rapidly growing animal.

Most of the tryptophan that is absorbed is used to form vitamin B3 (niacin). Poor diet could be the cause of a possible vitamin deficiency, or the body may be unable to absorb it, which can lead to the brain not receiving enough tryptophan to be able to make serotonin. Formation of serotonin depends on B6, another B vitamin, and folic acid (also a B vitamin) is probably also involved in this process. From this we can conclude that dogs that do not get enough of the various B vitamins, that cannot absorb B vitamins or that require a higher dose than usual because of stress, are able to form less serotonin. However, I would like to emphasise that this is purely speculation. Only the results of future research will be able to give a definitive answer. In practice it has been proven that dogs are much calmer and more balanced when they are given a vitamin B preparation (see list on page 120).

Just as a dog can be given insufficient food or be unable to make proper use of it, dogs may also be given unsuitable food. The issue of raw food – whether dogs should eat raw fish or cereal and which meat is the best – is a subject under constant debate at the moment. It is difficult, if not impossible, to take a clear stance here and each dog owner should decide what is best for their pet.

As mentioned earlier, cereals contain large quantities of the amino acid tyrosine, the precursor of the stress hormone noradrenaline. Tyrosine competes with tryptophan and can lead to an imbalance in stressed dogs. If your dog is anxious, aggressive, hyperactive or difficult to control, you should check whether their feed has a high cereal content.

Just as it should be – a trusting relationship between child and dog

Diseases and injuries

Illnesses can cause stress in different ways. Depending on what is wrong with the dog, the effect can range from mild to extreme stress.

Illnesses and various degrees of pain are obviously stressful for dogs, whatever their age. A dog that is often ill will experience more stress than one that is rarely ill. An ill dog does not just have pain to worry about. Visits to the vet may frighten her and cause more pain, depending on what happens in the surgery.

It is not just veterinary procedures that terrify dogs. Many puppies go into shock when they

Adult dogs are always important role models for puppies

are tattooed on their ears, stomach or inner thigh (since the advent of the microchip, tattooing has mercifully largely become a thing of the past). The same applies to clipping the nails, for example if they are cut too short or if the nail bed, where nerves and blood vessels are located, is damaged, or if the dog is forcibly held during clipping.

Other causes of stress

Apart from the stress factors for puppies described above, there are all kinds of stress factors that also affect adult dogs. These may include the behaviour of the family and their relationship with the dog, how neighbours and others behave towards him and what his environment is like, for example if a lot of children live in the neighbourhood, if there are frequent shots or bangs, if the dog regularly meets other dogs he does not get on with and many more. Many events may influence the dog, including possible trauma or the way that people work with the dog and, in particular, whether the dog is raised in a very authoritarian or a gentler way. A generous environment with effective and sensitive training causes less stress and can even improve tolerance to stress.

HORMONES

This includes hormones that change at puberty and the increased masculinity in more and more breeds that we have already mentioned. We

Sheep dogs are in their element when they can go about their work

should not forget that testosterone can also be a possible stress hormone. The effect of stress hormones (for example thyroid hormones) and stress reactions are also influenced by heredity.

THE ROLE MODEL

Our own influence as an example for the dog also cannot be ignored. Other role models are the dogs that our dog meets. There is a plausible correlation between authoritarian, punitive dog owners and the aggressive behaviour of their dogs towards other dogs. Closer examination is required here.

Depending on their disposition, other dogs in the family may teach negative behaviour. If a puppy bullies his siblings, he will probably treat other dogs in a similar manner later on.

The most common kinds of stress

There are so many unavoidable things in our environment that cause stress that we as dog owners should learn to recognise the most common stress factors for our dogs. Stress can be divided into strain, understimulation, insecurity, pain and shock.

STRAIN

A dog is put under strain when she is exposed to more stress factors than she is inherently able to process. For example, a harmless game can trigger negative stress when it is played with the dog too often and too vigorously. We should always keep in mind that excessive behaviour usually leads to negative stress. Playing a little is completely harmless, but it should always be just a game.

STRESS FACTORS THAT CAUSE STRAIN

Excessive use of the body, such as jumping, rapid acceleration and high speed, activates the "stress system" to increase physical strength temporarily. Playing too many hunting and fighting games runs the risk of straining the dog. For every bout of acceleration and every longer sprint, the brain sends impulses via the autonomic nervous system and through the hormones from the hypophysis, which leads to increased muscular strength.

The problem is that the performance of the dog's body is programmed by her ancestors' genes. Of course, wild canines have to accelerate and run, especially when hunting, but the question is, how often?

Wild canine species have always used their body's reserves for hunting, but hunts take place relatively infrequently, on average maybe once a week, sometimes more, sometimes less. It all depends on the skills of the prey and how easily it can be caught.

Wolves, the dog's closest relation, usually hunt the weakest animals, because they do not want to waste unnecessary energy hunting healthy, strong prey. In the winter there are fewer opportunities for hunting and success dwindles. The spring brings with it more huntable animals, although wolves prefer small rodents and helpless animals, because their capture uses up the least energy.

That means that dogs are programmed not to overexert themselves too often, perhaps just once or twice a week. Therefore, dogs cannot tolerate fetching or hunting games every day

or perhaps even every other day. Of course, individuals and breeds will differ. However, dogs of some hunting breeds and some sheepdogs react with stress when these situations are repeated too often and too intensively.

If the daily (or twice daily) throwing of sticks, balls and other objects that need to be fetched is repeated more than a few times in a row, the "stress machinery" becomes overstimulated. The behaviour is similar to the sudden acceleration and pursuit of fleeing prey. The same applies to playing with other dogs. If you watch dogs playing, it is clear that they are hunting each other – one dog plays the prey and the other the hunter and the roles are reversed frequently.

The adrenal gland becomes enlarged in animals that are overstimulated over a long period and it constantly produces elevated stress hormones.

I had a case involving a stressed German shepherd dog. I could tell that the dog was overstimulated, but the owner said that he never threw balls or sticks and that the dog did not play much with others. I asked about this several times, but the owner said that he knew it was not good for the dog. Just as I was about ready to give up, I asked one last question, "So you don't throw anything for your dog to fetch?" The owner replied, "Well of course he loves playing Frisbee and we do it every day." That was the explanation for the stress.

The same goes for tug-of-war and fighting games. They put strain on the body that activates the entire stress system. It does not matter when they actually happen, but games like this should not be played daily or every other day. Here is a warning about fighting games. Because they are

Prey games should not be played too often

an aggressive form of play, they can trigger too much aggressive behaviour in the dog. Most dogs enjoy pulling on a rag, shaking it and growling. It only becomes cause for concern when it happens too often and perhaps also in so-called "fighting breeds".

UNDERSTIMULATION

The most common cause of understimulation is boredom or far too little for the dog to do. Let's think about the origins of our dogs. They are the descendants of active, hunting animals. Their ancestors were active both physically and mentally, simply in order to survive. Prey animals are difficult to catch and even more difficult to kill. Every hunt is a major and sometimes dan-

gerous challenge and depends on the skill of the hunter, not just with regard to physical strength but also intelligence.

Dogs are pack animals, so they coordinate their behaviour. They are simultaneously active and passive. Often the mother or father in the pack takes the initiative for certain activities, such as moving on or hunting. When an action begins, the rest of the family follow the pack leader. When the leader is tired and lies down, so do the rest of the pack. This synchronisation of activities is practical because it means that all of the individuals have the same amount of energy at the same time.

Unfortunately, modern society no longer works like this. Instead it is quite the opposite.

Boredom or exhaustion?

We are relatively quiet and passive in the house. A young dog will follow us everywhere, but by the time he is a year old, he will have learned that this is boring and tiring. Nothing happens!

So the dog adapts and starts lying down. He rests and spends most of the day and night gathering energy. When he finally goes outside, the excess of energy is so great that the dog becomes hyperactive and exhibits various behavioural problems.

For many dogs, walks are boring and often consist of nothing more than wandering around, maybe with a little sniffing and leg-lifting. Not exactly a mental challenge for an animal as intelligent as a dog! It is not unusual for dogs to rest for 21 or 22 hours every day. There are even dogs that rest for more than 23 hours in a 24-hour day.

ESSENTIAL STIMULATION

Animals and people need to experience things in three ways: through the senses, through cognitive experiences and through social contact, but even too much of these can cause stress. Physical exercise is another experience that contributes to wellbeing.

Sensory impressions are a mix of visual experiences, different sounds, feelings – including physical contact – and scents. Scents are particularly important, because dogs live in a world full of important smells. Cognitive experiences include mental activities such as problem

Social contact with other dogs is important

solving, following a scent, finding objects and other challenges. Just as people enjoy games and puzzles, dogs need mental exercise to feel happy. Such stimulation can support brain growth, whereas too little stimulation allows the brain to shrink and lose weight. Furthermore, the number of dendrites, which are extensions of the nerve cells in the brain, decreases, leading to reduced intellectual capacity.

Social contact is extremely important from puppyhood onwards. Animals that grow up without contact with adults of the same species will be mentally and socially stunted for the rest of their life.

Social contact is particularly important for dogs. They have to get along with us, as well as with other members of their own species. It does not matter if the partners have two legs or four, the main thing is that they coexist well together. You cannot leave a dog alone for a whole day or shut him away in a kennel for days

Suckling releases oxytocin both in the young and in their mother and creates an emotional bond between them. Massage also promotes the formation of oxytocin, the basis for pleasant experiences.

Every dog needs security and physical contact

on end and expect him not to have any behavioural problems.

A dog needs company, security and physical contact. This was an important part of their ancestors' life for millennia and is still important today. They are family-orientated pack animals whose togetherness makes them stronger and who maintain physical contact in different ways. A friendly touch is perceived as being positive and prevents stress, both in people and in dogs. It gives young animals security and strengthens the bond between adults. Positive physical contact causes oxytocin, a brain chemical that calms and is experienced as positive, to be released. When you stroke your dog, oxytocin is released both in you and in your dog. It is probably the physiological basis for positive experiences.

BOREDOM AND CORTISOL

Monotony is often associated with the adrenal gland stress hormone cortisol, which creates mental tension as well as unpleasant sensations. Even if a sleeping dog looks relaxed, power is being built up inside, like a volcano shortly before it erupts.

The antidote is simple – challenge the body and mind. There are simple ways to activate a dog immediately (see *Mental Training for Your Dog*, Hallgren, 2007). It often only takes a week for an understimulated dog to become balanced.

INSECURITY

In dogs, insecurity is caused by early experiences when they were not in control and were not able to predict their owner's reactions or to know what was going to happen next. Everything in their life is unpredictable. Sometimes nothing happens; sometimes something very unpleasant happens. Sometimes the owner is in a good mood; sometimes not. Sometimes the dog is allowed on the sofa; sometimes he is not.

Uncertainty and confusion are so normal in life that insecurity is the order of the day. Oddly enough, most dogs, or at least those that are well cared for, appear to be able to avoid excessive stress caused by uncertainty.

Dogs that are not well cared for exhibit many stress symptoms such as aggression, fear and other behavioural problems. There are tragic cases where the dog is afraid of their owner and extremely submissive. Contradictory actions can also make a dog very insecure.

This is often the case in dogs with authoritarian owners or owners who suffer from mood swings or social problems. Owners that dominate dogs with orders and punishment often have insufficient knowledge and empathy. In cases like this, the dog loses the feeling that he is able to control the situations that he faces. He constantly has to follow orders and does not know what he may and may not do.

Unfortunately, this authoritative attitude is taught by some television programmes, books and articles about dogs. Problem behaviour is "fixed" using punishment and the case is argued for passive and obedient dogs. In other words, viewers and readers are taught that dogs may not control themselves, but must be under control.

Early trauma can lead to insecurity

However, we can have full control over our dogs without taking away their sense of using their own initiative and having free will. It all depends on how we raise, educate and train our dogs and how great the demands are that we place on them.

MANY THINGS CAN MAKE A DOG INSECURE

Making fun of a dog can make her insecure. Dogs do not understand tricks or teasing, so they cannot understand the result of a relatively stressful, uncontrollable situation. For example, there are dog owners who pretend that there is somebody coming to the door, just to see how their dog runs to the door and raises the alarm. For some inexplicable reason they find this to be funny.

A dog may refuse to cooperate if you deal with him the wrong way

Laughing at a dog often leads to submissive signals. The dog does not understand why he is the focus of people who are showing their teeth and making strange noises.

Domestic disputes are another "hidden" stress factor. Dogs react sensitively to hard, loud and very shrill voices. Most of them associate this with negative outcomes, perhaps combined with threats or pain if they have done something wrong. When family members argue, they are obviously focused on each other and do not notice the dog slinking away with submissive body language, tail down and ears flat. The dog probably thinks that she is the one being scolded. If you must argue please do not do it in the presence of your dog!

Life without routine is unpredictable. Dogs have to have some idea of what is going on. If they cannot predict various situations they become insecure. This includes everyday occurrences such as:

- Not actually going out when the owner puts on their coat or says that it is time for a walk
- Being shut in when something happens in which the dog cannot participate
- Not being fed at feeding time when the bowls have been brought out
- Being shut out and not being allowed in the car when everybody else drives away
- The owner tells their dog that somebody is coming "for fun" and that person does not materialise

An insecure dog is usually withdrawn

Dogs become insecure in situations in which they do not understand their owner's threats, force or aggression, for example if a dog:

- Is called and then punished because he did not come quickly enough
- Is verbally reprimanded in a threatening voice for something that he could do, for example another dog growls and barks and the dog is punished because he too might growl and bark
- Is kept on too short a lead when he passes an unknown dog (which frequently happens at shows), because this is forced social contact where the appropriate body language signals cannot be given first
- Is treated badly by his owner because he did not do well in a competition
- Is treated badly because his owner is in a bad mood
- Always hears a "no"
- Is never given any attention

Unfortunately, this list could be much longer, so please have a good look at your own behaviour. Your relationship with your dog will determine his behaviour, his wellbeing and his contentment.

THE PACK IS SO IMPORTANT ...

Social life is very important for pack animals. It provides security and protection against danger, as well as play and care. Cooperation

Nose–body contact takes place quite often in packs

when hunting, for example, increases the chance of finding and killing prey. Social life is so important that some canine behaviour encourages cohesion and communication between pack members. You could say that dogs use this behaviour to work on their relationships.

For example, nose–body contact can be observed frequently in canines, either wolves or dogs. Erik Zimen found out that, in a wolf pack, nose–fur contact took place on average six times an hour during migration. This contact encourages cohesion and makes communication between individuals easier.

Greeting rituals fulfil the same purpose. Intensive communication, when pack members meet after sleeping or after they have been apart, strengthens emotional and social bonds.

However, we should remember that individual wild pack animals, such as wolves, can leave the group at any time. If they are unhappy or if there is too much rivalry within the family, they go their own way, find a new territory and maybe a partner, in order to start a new family. Unfortunately, domestic dogs do not have this option.

... BUT IT CAN ALSO BE NEGATIVE

It has been shown that overpopulation and the resulting social confrontation is stressful for animals, as well as for people. The more mice that live together in a small space, the higher the incidence of stress-induced illnesses such as high blood pressure, heart problems and aggression. Overpopulation increases the release of stress hormones and leads to enlargement of the adrenal gland, which produces stress hormones.

Stress caused by overpopulation can occur if too many dogs are kept in cramped conditions for a long time. The situation can arise when a family has several dogs and it can even become dangerous if the dogs do not like each other. Being kept in a kennel for a long time can result in stress symptoms caused by overpopulation. The risk can also be increased, for example by overcrowding, conflicts within the group, new admissions that change the pecking order, and separation by age, breed and health.

Stress is therefore not just determined by the number of individual animals per unit area. For example, dogs can cope with spending entire days at crowded dog shows, but they are admittedly totally exhausted when they come home. They may need 24 hours of sleep to recover. They seem to be able to tolerate temporary overcrowding in the same way that we can tolerate temporary stressful situations.

In this context, it is worth mentioning how few fights there are when so many dogs are brought together in a small space. Perhaps the crowd itself is what holds them back. A fight would involve all of the individuals gathered, and the dogs seem to recognise this. Perhaps they also stay calm because they are on other dogs' territory. They cannot know which animals live in and control the new territory they have entered, and it might be all of the other dogs there. However, there is one thing that each dog knows: it is not my territory.

AUTHORITY IN EDUCATION AND TRAINING

There are many different ways of training dogs, from gentle to coercive. Pet dogs are normally trained gently using modern methods, while hunting dogs are commonly trained with severity and force.

In this respect, dogs in Scandinavia are better off than dogs in other parts of the world. With a few exceptions in the training of hunting dogs, the use of electric shock devices is banned in Sweden, Norway and Denmark. Criticism of this method is based both on its effects and on the way in which the handler may deal with the dog, as the following example shows.

A Dutch study investigated the effect of electric shock collars and compared it with the effect seen in dogs that did not receive an electric shock, but were trained using physical violence, in which they were kicked, struck and pulled by a prong collar.

The study showed that the dogs that were given electric shocks were more stressed than the others. They associated the electric shock with the trainers and became afraid of them. This effect was extended into all situations, not just training. So many changes in behaviour occurred associated with the electric shocks that the dogs' health was considered to be at risk.

In 1989, the Norwegian magazine *Jakt & Fiske* (*Hunting & Fishing*) published an evaluation of an investigation in which 568 dogs that had chased sheep were trained with an electric shock collar. The result was an improvement in 78 percent, which is low for such a brutal method. Furthermore, the differences between individual breeds were great, with German shepherd dogs being the worst pupils – around 67 percent continued to chase sheep after training. The result was 100 percent in hunting dogs, probably because they are more sensitive.

Chasing sheep or other animals is not desired in most dogs

Around a third of all of the dogs showed behavioural changes: 27 percent were cautious and showed avoidance behaviour. A little over 30 percent became afraid of sheep, which was regarded as positive from the trainer's point of view. Only around half of the owners reported that their dogs had actually stopped chasing sheep altogether. Furthermore, the fear of sheep did not transfer to other hoofed animals such as deer.

The result was considered to be good for people who used their dogs for hunting, but bad for those who kept pet dogs that were not supposed to hunt at all.

ILLNESS AND PAIN

Illness and pain are stress factors that are very often underestimated and that occur more frequently than we might think. Just like people, dogs can suffer from toothache, headache, fever caused by infections, stomach ache, painful wounds, joint pain, muscular pain, problems with seeing and hearing, and many more.

Many people believe that dogs have a very high pain threshold and are seldom ill. Neither of these assertions is true. Measurements have shown that pain is the most common cause of behavioural problems in dogs. Of the "normal" dog population, 60 percent have back problems, and that speaks volumes. If you count breed-specific illnesses, contagious diseases and injuries, the probability that a given dog is ill or in pain is very high.

The biggest problem with sick dogs is that we usually cannot tell from their facial expression that they are ill. For some inexplicable reason, we humans expect dogs to show us their pain in the same way that we do, with sounds and facial expressions. However, that is not the case. Most animals hardly show any signs of being in pain, apart from small changes in their expression, so it is very hard for us to believe that our dog is ill.

What's more, she is playing and jumping about, so she must be healthy. Wrong! A dog can be very ill and in great pain, but when something exciting happens, the pain is temporarily forgotten. We react in exactly the same way.

ACUTE STRESS REACTION

Acute stress reaction (shock) is a sudden and complete overloading of the nervous system. Behavioural changes such as anxiety, nervousness and tension usually follow an acute stress reaction. It is easier for older dogs to recover, but in puppies and young dogs acute stress reaction often leads to permanent behavioural disorders. Unfortunately, these changes are difficult and sometimes impossible to rectify by training alone. A typical reaction can be a terror of certain things, people or sounds. As well as behavioural changes, acute stress reaction also causes changes in the hormone balance and the nervous system.

These common and long-lasting effects of acute stress reaction are described as post-traumatic stress disorder (PTSD).

The acute stress reaction or psychological trauma is divided into three different phases.

- The first phase is the acute trauma that follows the stress reaction immediately. The dog is deeply upset and disorientated. He often does not hear what is said to him and does not seem able to take in information.
- The second phase begins when the acute stress reaction or its effects do not subside. The dog does not seem to be functioning properly. This is described as a chronic or extended stress reaction. The affected dog is shaken. He panics at times when he used to be cool, calm and collected and tends towards aggressive outbursts when he would have been composed and quiet before.
- The third phase is described as the latent stress reaction. This is the phase where the dog appears to have returned to his normal behaviour, except when something happens that reminds him of the shock. For example, if a dog has been hit by a car, he does not show any fear of cars or most roads, but reacts with panic at the stretch of road where he was run over.

Different dogs react in different ways when they have traumatic experiences. Some become extremely nervous; others do not. Some come to terms with the experience in a short time; others will be affected by it for the rest of their life. The actual causes probably occurred far back in time, even as far back as puppyhood. Heredity and age also play a role.

SYMPTOMS

All traumatic events lead to behavioural changes, to a lesser or greater extent. These

Fear and insecurity are often the result of trauma

mainly include emotional disturbances such as uncontrollable outbursts of fear, irritability or aggression, but sometimes also shyness and restlessness, and in severe cases depression and apathy.

Symptoms also include sleep disorders. The animal feels so insecure that any form of relaxation means a kind of danger. Sleep is characterised by fear and frequent dreams. Dogs will often look for a particularly safe place to sleep, such as under a table, in a cupboard or in a corner.

Another symptom is that different types of behaviour are blocked. If a dog used to greet other dogs, sniffed them, wanted to impress them, approached them on stiff legs and finally played with them, only some components of this behaviour will now occur. The original ritual may have been replaced with growling and submission. The dog's earlier achievements in obedience and tracking work are no longer as good. The dog loses her confidence and cannot concentrate as well.

It is often found that somebody who has suffered a shock reacts more strongly to subsequent disruptions and, in particular, to sudden events. A dog that has had a traumatic experience will be more easily intimidated than a dog that has not had such a trauma. If she is threatened she will be much angrier than before the trauma. She appears to be moodier and more easily irritated.

Pacification is a common behaviour shown by insecure dogs

LACK OF CONCENTRATION

You can often tell when a dog has had an acute stress reaction. He seems tense, restless, jittery and stressed and appears to constantly be checking his environment as if searching for possible danger. The dog immediately notices people that approach him and concentrates fully on following their movements.

The dog is so nervous that he jumps up at every sudden noise. He is unable to concentrate for more than a short period of time. Even when assessing and sniffing a scent mark, he keeps on raising his head to check on his surroundings, like guard dog. His tail will often be clamped between his legs and he will listen for possible dangers with his ears lying flat. Increased

sensitivity to sounds is also typical in dogs that have had a traumatic experience.

CAUTION

Perhaps one of the most striking features of a traumatised dog is that she appears to expect unpleasant things and negative experiences. Above all, she anticipates unpleasant experiences in new and unfamiliar places. She does not like to enter an unfamiliar room without first investigating it slowly and carefully from the doorway.

A strangely shaped object, such as a paper bag, that is normally not on the usual path can both frighten and entice her. The dog cannot leave the area without investigating the bag

Traumatised dogs often hide away

first. When she does so, she stretches and tenses each muscle so that she is ready for flight. She crouches down as she approaches the object. The danger is over when she has sniffed the object and made sure that it is harmless.

EARLY TRAUMAS ARE THE WORST

Puppies are extremely sensitive and a single trauma can have devastating consequences. If a puppy has an acute stress reaction, it usually leads to a permanent and severe change both in their personality and in their behaviour. The puppy's entire approach to their environment, their experiences, their emotional state and their ability to learn can be influenced.

An older dog that has experienced a trauma will specifically be afraid of what he remembers, but traumatised puppies will be afraid of everything unknown to them. The shock can be so generalised that it influences the puppy's entire world of experience.

FIREWORKS AS A SEVERE TRAUMA

Trauma is the most extreme stress reaction. It is so intense that it can even result in death. It is relatively common for dogs to die in the first three weeks of January – after the New Year celebration – because of heart failure. They have been so badly traumatised by fireworks that it is comparable to the experience of soldiers who are bombarded in war.

One family took their five-month-old German shepherd dog to a Guy Fawkes Night party with a bonfire. Many of the people there greeted their friendly and well-socialised young dog. Suddenly, and less than seven metres away, the advertised fireworks began. Rockets flew to the nearby lake. The dog showed signs of stress. She was uneasy about the banging, whooshing and whistling of the fireworks. Somebody threw a firecracker into the bon-fire, which gave off a sound like a machine gun, right next to the dog, who was not used to loud bangs. She panicked and, although her owners tried to calm her down, they did not leave the party. This firework produced an acute stress reaction in the dog.

Ever since that day the dog has been unable to go to places in which there is more than one person. She is afraid of strangers, extremely sensitive to sound and is very cautious in strange surroundings. Her appetite changed and she only came into heat for the first time at two years old. In short, she grew from a happy puppy into a passive, anxious dog.

Treatment and healing

*N*owadays it is possible to treat stress, anxiety and aggression successfully in dogs. The prognosis is quite good when compared to the situation 25 years ago. You can find practical instructions for treatment and healing in this chapter. If you follow these instructions you will have a good chance of being able to help your dog. There are also instructions on how to deal with a traumatised dog. Interestingly, positive results can often be achieved with the right food.

Solving a problem successfully, dealing with a threatening situation in the right way or having the energy to stand up to pressure boosts self-confidence.

The feeling of being in control of a situation is another positive factor and it is important because it diminishes the effects of a stress reaction.

An example is a dog that finds it difficult to be shut alone in a room. He whines, runs around and scratches and jumps up at the door. At some point the dog manages to move the door handle and open the door. He has put all of his energy into solving the problem in this situation, which he perceived to be intolerable.

Predictability and the feeling of being in control

When an animal (or a human being) is suddenly exposed to, and perhaps even traumatised by, an unpleasant situation, they respond with a powerful stress reaction in which they may react with panic, attack or paralysis. An animal will often urinate or defecate and scream out of pure fear.

However, if the animal knows how to deal with this situation, the reaction is not as extreme. You could say that the animal can predict what will happen. It has time to prepare for it and the situation does not come as such

Freezing is a sign of passive resignation

a surprise, instead, it is more a matter of "gritting your teeth". Animals feel that they are in control if they can also do something to prevent or at least reduce the shock. This stabilises them mentally and gives them more confidence (at least in certain situations).

In an experiment, three groups of rats were confronted with electric shocks. One group could not predict when the shock was coming, but received it without warning. The second group was given the same electric shock, but received a warning signal shortly before each shock. The third group was the control group and did not receive any shocks. The rats that were given electric shocks without warning

and therefore could not predict them developed ulcers and many other serious signs of stress. The rats that were warned in advance exhibited few or no stress symptoms, and were almost the same as the control group.

In order to find out the effect of the ability to control situations, the same researchers taught a group of rats how to switch the electricity on or off using a wheel. The wheel's lever was removed after the rats had learned how to use it. This meant that the electric shocks could no longer be prevented. The rats lost control of the situation and showed various signs of stress.

Being part of a group gives dogs security

DOGS AND HELPLESSNESS

Martin Seligman achieved comparable results in similar experiments with dogs. This experiment took place in the 1970s and will not be described in detail here. Nowadays the use of dogs in a test set-up with electric shocks would be unthinkable. Below is a brief comment on the results:

Dogs that were exposed to a stressful situation that they could not control developed illnesses caused by stress, such as ulcers, immunodeficiency, cardiac problems, as well as many psychological signs such as fear, timidity, aggression, avoidance behaviour, passivity, eating disorders and many more. They developed a kind of passive resignation that was described as "learned helplessness".

The dogs had learned that there was no way to escape the situation. Passive helplessness followed them for the rest of their lives. Both their behaviour and their physical condition changed. They became passive, submissive, evasive, antisocial and they stopped playing. In many cases their appetite changed, their coat became poor, their immune system weakened and their life expectancy decreased.

THE NEED TO CONTROL

Dogs like to be in control of their situation, especially in a strange environment, but also at home. The social environment is very important for many dogs, especially if they live in a human family, but also if they have been brought together with other dogs.

Dogs need social contact and the feeling of belonging to a group, and they like to get to know each other if they meet regularly. Many believe that this shows the requirement for a strong bond and a strict pecking order, but modern behavioural researchers and biologists are now questioning the whole hierarchy concept. The simplest explanation is that dogs simply want to get to know one another and perhaps build up mutual trust.

ENCOUNTERING NEW SITUATIONS

When an individual is getting to know a new environment and new members of the same species, it is normal for certain stress reactions to occur. This enables dogs to cope mentally and physically if something should go wrong, if danger awaits them in a new environment, or if an unknown dog is aggressive. If a dog is anxious and submissive when she encounters new situations, more cortisol is released. If she is successful, gets the situation under control and is not exposed to any threats or danger, more adrenaline is produced.

The ability to predict and control stressful events is therefore crucial for the development of the stress experience. If somebody can control a difficult situation, such as physical trauma or a frightening experience, such situations do not stress them as much.

If a serious situation occurs without warning, such as a sudden thunder clap very close by, a sudden attack from behind, or unprovoked aggression from another dog, a dog can have an acute stress reaction.

Something can turn into a traumatic experience if it is not possible to predict what will happen. Had there been any kind of prior warning, the dog would have had the chance to prepare for it mentally and would probably have been able to control the situation that has now led to a traumatic experience.

RECOGNITION EFFECT

A dog that has never heard a firework before can be severely traumatised when the loud bangs start on bonfire night or at the New Year. The recognition effect comes in when the dog has already heard these sounds from a distance or has had them played to him on a CD. This is similar to predictability, because the dog already knows these sounds and can brace himself mentally for the bangs and the whole process. However, if it gets too much, because the banging sounds are too close, for example, the dog loses the feeling that he has control over the situation.

Overcoming a situation

How well a dog (or a human being) can manage a difficult situation depends on how great the stress factor in the situation is. How well an animal can deal with a situation determines whether or not they can tolerate the stress.

There are two ways of managing difficulties. You either fight or flee, or remain completely passive and avoid confrontation. Some deal actively with stress; others would rather adapt, but this comes at a high price. Both strategies can be successful, although they differ

An example of active coping in an unpleasant situation

Active coping leads to activation of the sympathetic portion of the autonomic nervous system. The adrenaline-producing system is active, while the cortisol-producing system is inactive. Passive coping leads to activation of the parasympathetic portion of the autonomic nervous system. Cortisol is released. The main function of the parasympathetic system is to synthesise nutrients and to support the recovery phase.

in effort and cost. They are called active and passive coping and are controlled by different parts of the autonomic nervous system.

ACTIVE COPING

Active coping involves confrontation, and the mobilisation of energy reserves in an active attempt to adapt to the possible event through fight or flight. The "event" could be the approach of an unknown dog in a threatening manner. The stress system switches up into a higher gear to be prepared for everything that could happen.

In this case, the dog fights to get the situation under control. She is ready, physically and mentally. The dog does not intend to let herself be bitten. She tries to get out of the way of the other dog using resistance or flight. This

Submission is an example of passive coping

is described as active coping. The dog tries to manage the situation by taking action using fight or flight.

PASSIVE COPING

In passive coping, a dog will not tend towards an aggressive reaction. If an unknown, threatening dog approaches, the dog will avoid taking any risks if at all possible, either by evading the situation or submitting. He appears to have accepted that he cannot control the situation. These animals are the quieter representatives of type B.

BOTH STRATEGIES ARE POSSIBLE

Genetic makeup, age and life experience from birth until this moment determine whether a

dog overcomes this kind of situation actively or passively. However, any dog can resort to either strategy and the choice depends on the situation.

Dogs that have suffered from learned helplessness their whole life, as a result of ill treatment, have learned that they cannot do anything to improve or change a situation. These dogs have only one strategy. They seem to have given up, because they endure pain without trying to fight back. The same phenomenon can be observed in victims of domestic abuse and other people in similar situations.

WHICH STRATEGY DOES YOUR DOG USE?

Perhaps you know now which strategy your dog prefers in most situations and whether she copes with situations actively or passively. Can she deal with threats, and does she have the confidence to investigate something unknown? Is she fearless and confident when exposed to new situations or does she run away? Does she submit when she is threatened? Does she investigate unknown things or does she avoid them? Is she cautious or hesitant with something that she has not experienced before? Is she quiet and balanced in a social environment, especially when meeting other dogs?

If your dog is traumatised

A dog can easily have a traumatic experience. He could be frightened by a careless person, a backfiring car or children throwing firecrackers nearby. A dog can also have a painful experience at the veterinary clinic. A wasp sting or a dog that attacks without warning can also cause an acute stress reaction. These are all

The effects of an acute stress reaction can last for a very long time. Severe and prolonged stress weakens the immune system, which results in a higher risk of infection. The strain on internal organs such as the heart and digestive system increases the risk of illness. Furthermore, an imbalance between the chemical messengers in the brain may occur.

examples from my everyday working life.

Years of research into the consequences of shock in dogs have taught me that timing is the most important factor. The consequences of trauma can be greatly reduced and limited if the right treatment is given as promptly as possible. That does not mean that the effects of a traumatic experience that took place long ago cannot be healed, but it is more difficult.

TREATMENT OF ACUTE STRESS REACTION

If your dog has been traumatised, you should make sure that she receives some sort of sedative as soon as possible, preferably within 24 hours. It can be a herbal remedy from a wholefood shop or supermarket or medication from a vet.

Do not administer sedatives when your dog is still in a state of shock and if the oral mucous membranes are pale. Contact your vet immediately if your dog is still experiencing an acute stress reaction.

Follow the dosage recommended by your vet or stated on the packing of the herbal remedy! If you are unsure about the appropriate remedy, ask a specialist, such as a herbalist or a dog psychologist who specialises in behavioural problems. They can give you more information about other treatments that could help your dog. Bear in mind that reactions to herbal remedies differ from dog to dog.

Supplement the treatment with a vitamin B complex and DAP (dog appeasing pheromone, the synthetic version of the tranquilising hormones produced by bitches after giving birth). The latter can be sprayed in a room for a calming effect.

If your dog has not calmed down within a week, you should contact a trained canine behaviourist.

Acute shock can be treated with sedatives

Continue the treatment for acute stress reaction for around three to four weeks and then reduce the sedative dose gradually. Slowly reduce the vitamin B complex dosage, but give your dog a small dose of vitamin B for a further

If your dog has had a severe shock, always get your vet to prescribe a sedative that can be administered over the longest possible time.

four or five months. You will also have to work with your dog during this time.

TREATMENT AFTER A SHOCK OR TREATMENT OF PERSISTENT STRESS

An acute stress reaction or long lasting stress will cause a dog to require more food than normal. This is because the body's energy reserves have been depleted by the increased concentration of stress hormones, which raises the risk of malnutrition. Because the body is using up large quantities of vitamin B complex and certain minerals, I would recommend administering a B-50 vitamin complex, as in the treatment of acute stress reaction. Ask your vet if you are unsure about the dosage. The risk of overdose

The treatment must be adapted to the size of the dog

is not high, but if your dog develops diarrhoea, reduce the dose.

Give your dog a valerian preparation for around two months following an acute stress reaction. The dose should be around half that given for immediate treatment of an acute stress reaction. If your vet gives you Inderal or a similar preparation, it makes training easier because it has a sedative effect.

Other options for treating your dog should be discussed with your vet.

CHANGES IN THE BRAIN

An imbalance may occur in the chemical messengers in the brain following a shock or long-term stress. As mentioned earlier on, stress affects noradrenaline and serotonin, among other messengers.

Post-traumatic treatment must be continued for five or six months, or even up to a year for a serious acute stress response. The dog's intake of nutrients must be adequate (vitamins, especially vitamin B, and minerals are important). Preparations that support the formation of serotonin have a particularly positive effect.

Serotonin is formed from the amino acid tryptophan, large quantities of which can be found in turkey meat, brown rice, bananas, spinach, pumpkin seeds and milk. (This is why the old trick of having a glass of milk before bedtime to make you calm and sleepy works.) The addition of vitamin B6 (pyridoxine) is important because it has a supportive effect.

Vitamin B3 (niacin) is mainly formed in the body by tryptophan; 60 parts of tryptophan are needed to make one part of niacin. However, the body cannot rely on tryptophan alone. It also needs vitamins B3 and B6. Supplementation with a B-vitamin complex is the most effective. The quantity normally depends on the size and weight of the dog. It is best to give your dog a vitamin B complex that covers all of the B vitamins.

Seek advice from your vet if your dog cannot calm down after an acute stress reaction.

How tryptophan becomes serotonin:
Tryptophan > 5-Hydroxytryptophan > 5-Hydroxytryptamine = 5-HTP = Serotonin.

The seeds of the African plant *Griffonia*

simplicifolia are made into the intermediate 5-hydroxytryptophan. It is regarded as the fastest and safest substance available for this purpose and is suitable for very anxious dogs. The product is available under the name 5-HTP.
Caution:
Avoid overdose!
The preparation should only be administered following discussion with your vet.

From the weak to the strong

The amount of tryptophan that you administer to your dog depends on how much he has been traumatised. If the dog only has mild symptoms and becomes slightly stressed in certain situations, but is otherwise balanced, you can give him the B-50 complex, as well as dried bananas, soya protein or dried turkey (whatever your dog prefers), now and then. If he is not too fussy you can also mix a little spinach into his food.

You can spoil your dog with treats made from dried turkey meat (simply dry the meat in the oven at a low temperature) and banana chips (available in the snack aisle of your supermarket). However, do not give him any milk, because dogs are lactose intolerant and milk quickly upsets their stomachs.

If your dog is easily stressed in various situations and has poor impulse control, give him the B-50 complex and mix a few pumpkin seeds into his feed every day. Start off with small quantities so that your dog can get used to the taste, then increase the quantity to around one-fifth of a teaspoon for a toy breed such as a Chihuahua or Yorkshire terrier, half a teaspoon for a small dog such as a Jack Russell terrier, a teaspoon for a medium-sized dog such as a cocker spaniel, two teaspoons or a tablespoon for a large dog such as a Labrador retriever or one and a half or two tablespoons for a giant breed such as a Great Dane.

If the dog is nervous, anxious or aggressive, has hardly any impulse control, becomes totally blocked in various situations and has therefore been stressed by one or more traumatic experiences, you can administer a special tryptophan preparation. However, you should seek the advice of somebody with experience of treatment of post-traumatic stress.

Sedatives containing various concentrations of tryptophan are available especially for dogs and can be found in pet shops or on the Internet. Follow the manufacturer's dosage instructions or the recommendations of your vet.

For a dog that is extremely anxious, nervous or aggressive, has panic attacks and scarcely any impulse control, or that displays similar symptoms, I would recommend a certain substance, an intermediate product of the biosynthesis of tryptophan into serotonin (see Box on page 118), which is also available in wholefood shops. It is called 5-HTP (5-Hydroxytryptophan) and is made from an African plant. An overdose can be dangerous, so only give it to your dog following your vet's instructions. Administer the B-50 complex at the same time.

VITAMINS AND MINERALS

If you work together with an expert who has experience in the treatment of post-traumatic stress, you will probably give your dog extra vitamins and minerals, because a stressed dog's requirements are greater. However, you must consider what the dog eats and assess how many supplements she needs with her meals.

Experts in nutrition used to be hard to find, but special nutrition courses, as part of behavioural research courses, are now available in many countries. Make sure that the expert has completed this kind of course and that they know about feeding traumatised and stressed animals.

TYROSINE CAN COUNTERACT TRYPTOPHAN

Tyrosine is also an amino acid, and it is a precursor of adrenaline, noradrenaline and dopamine.

Tyrosine competes with tryptophan to penetrate nerve cells and can therefore decrease the quantity of tryptophan available, which in turn inhibits the formation of serotonin. Tyrosine is found mainly in cereals, so you should make sure that your dog's food does not contain too high a percentage. Protein, found in meat for example, is also rich in tyrosine and should be balanced out with carbohydrates.

You should seek professional advice if your dog has not recovered two or three weeks after the incident. Remember that all dogs can react differently to herbal remedies. Your dog will also need emotional support and perhaps retraining during this time.

The amino acid tryptophan (precurser of serotonin) is given to dogs to balance out the relationship between noradrenaline and serotonin.
The amino acid tyrosine is a precursor of adrenaline, noradrenaline and dopamine. It is present in cereals and animal proteins, among other foods, and competes with tryptophan to penetrate nerve cells. Therefore the food given to a stressed dog should not contain too much cereal or too much protein.

Sedatives for dogs	Supplier
Valerian products	Wholefood shops

Herbal medicines that contain serotonin, natural remedies and vitamins

5-HTP	Wholefood shops
Tryptophan (various brand names)	Wholefood shops
Zylkene	Vet
Serene-UM	Vet
Magnesium mix	Wholefood shops
St John's Wort preparations	Wholefood shops

Increases the availability of serotonin

- Side effects: make skin more sensitive to light – do not give to hairless dogs!
- Increased risk of haemorrhage: the vet must be informed that the dog has been given this kind of preparation before an operation.
- If the dog is in poor condition you must consult a vet before administering this medication.

This plant increases the breakdown of steroids and is also an alternative for treating extremely masculine male dogs.

Food and drinks that contain particularly large amounts of tryptophan

Banana (banana chips); single dose	Wholefood shops/supermarkets
Turkey meat; single dose or mix with food	Supermarket
Ground pumpkin seeds; less than stated by manufacturer*	Wholefood shops
Alcohol-free lager; add small quantities to food	Supermarket
Brown rice; mix into daily food	Supermarket
Soya protein; mix into daily food	Wholefood shops/supermarkets

Important vitamins

B vitamins (especially B3, B6 and folic acid)	Wholefood shops
½ to 1 tablet, depending on the size of the dog*	
Alternatively B-50 vitamin complex	

Others

SSRIs block serotonin receptors in the brain	
Clomicalm	Vet, on prescription only
DAP (pheromone); according to manufacturer's instructions	Vet/pharmacist

It is difficult to find the correct does for natural remedies, because every dog reacts differently. Always start with a small quantity and increase it gradually until the desired effect is achieved.

Young dogs often go through a phase when they are afraid of the unknown

The most important feeling is that you have everything under control

The difference between active and passive coping is, as mentioned above, that the active type reacts by fighting or fleeing, while the passive type tolerates or submits. Both strategies work, but in different ways.

Young dogs often go through an anxious phase (often described as the "fear of strangers phase") shortly before or during puberty. They are mainly afraid of the unknown. From the dog's point of view it could be a road sign in the dusk, a hanging sign that moves in the wind,

In character tests for dogs, a "ghost" will often appear in the form of a person hiding under a sheet, a bed sheet hanging from a tree or a pointing figure that is pulled on a slide in the direction of the dog. A character test is not a measure of genetic predisposition, but is used mainly to discover whether a dog reacts actively or passively.

The "ghost exercise" is part of a character test to determine how the dog reacts to the unknown

a stooping person picking berries in the forest, or a man who walks strangely or looks like a chimney sweep.

The active type reacts to something scary by growling or barking, but sooner or later curiosity gets the better of him and he approaches and sniffs the strange object. Or he runs away. This dog solves the problem actively.

The passive type stays at a distance, evades, avoids or freezes. He remains totally introverted. This behaviour is typical of a helpless dog that accepts the situation, but is absolutely petrified.

HELPLESSNESS CAN BE AVOIDED

It is important for a dog to develop a good strategy so that she is able to deal with stress. Dogs should be given environmental and so-

cial training, because the more a dog encounters different people, other dogs and different situations, the less stressed her reaction to new things in her life will be.

Authoritative education with a lot of punishment, requirements for extreme obedience, yanking on the lead, screaming and bawling make a dog passive and helpless. The age-old and unresolved conflict between soft and hard training rears its head again here. When stress appears, it is another important argument against the authoritarian treatment of dogs.

The more you hinder, dominate and control a dog, the more passive she becomes. If this is exaggerated, it results in learned helplessness, which can lead to depression.

Marianne Frankenhaeuser and Maj Ödman carried out an interesting experiment on this subject, using people. They investigated the importance of feeling in control when stressed by a crowd of people. They wanted to know whether the ability to take control decreases in a crowd. The experiment took place on a commuter train and concerned two groups – one group that was on the train from the beginning and another group that only boarded halfway into the journey. The passengers themselves evaluated how cramped, uneasy and stressed they felt and they each gave a urine sample so that stress hormone levels could be examined.

The results showed that the passengers who had been on the train for the whole journey were less stressed than those who had boarded halfway through. There was more space during the first half of the long journey and everybody could choose where they wanted to sit. Most of the seats were taken when the passengers joined halfway through. They could not choose a seat and many had to stand very close to other passengers.

Dogs want to communicate

Dogs pay for your control

The more you want to control your dog, the higher the price your dog will eventually have to pay in the form of submissiveness and passivity. He will have less freedom in the life you share together. If your dog is confronted constantly with restrictions and commands such as "no" and "go and lie down", he will be unable to communicate when he needs to go outside, point out that his water bowl is empty or express that something is very important for him. You have taught him that this is not allowed.

Dogs become passive easily

Dogs can quickly become passive, because they are pack animals. They adapt their behaviour to that of others, and often act on the initiative of other pack members. That is why dogs cooperate so well together, but it is also why they are so easily forced into passivity by simple control.

It is better to have a confident and active dog than one that is too obedient and passive. Dominated dogs take the initiative less, whereas dogs that grow up in a generous environment and are allowed to do more also take the initiative more. They can communicate better, they are more sociable, easier to motivate in training and happier.

It is no wonder that more and more modern trainers are using operant conditioning, which means that the dog has to find out for herself how to get a reward. That is one of the foundations for clicker training. It makes learning considerably more effective, but also fun.

There is good reason to criticise methods that are based on punishment and control. A dog cannot enjoy her work and be obedient if she loses something essential: her ability to take the initiative and, in the worst case, her enjoyment of life.

Training

Trauma or long-term stress increases the production of stress hormones by the adrenal gland. In turn, this increases blood flow in the muscles, oxygen intake and the release of fat and blood sugar, all of which strengthens the body.

After trauma or long-term stress, your dog will need a lot more exercise to work off his energy, so varied walks are an important part of treatment. Physical activity increases the absorption of blood sugar in the muscles. That is important in stopping the blood sugar level from rising. Exercise is recommended for people to prevent heart disease, depression, diabetes and anxiety, and the same applies to dogs.

Exercise should be varied. A combination of walking, trotting and little "gymnastic exercises" will raise the pulse slightly. A little game is good, but the dog should mainly use up his energy in a relaxed way. Acceleration releases stress hormones from the adrenal glands, so too much should be avoided in stress relief training. The right mix must be found for every

"Gymnastic exercises" should be incorporated into every walk

dog, depending on his breed and character. At the same time, walks must not be boring, but should include little exercises that make the dog think.

Regular physical exercise also influences the release of serotonin and endorphins, which makes it a pleasant experience for the dog.

Mental stimulation

Physical exercise is important, but mental stimulation is equally valuable for therapy. It boosts the dog's self-confidence and at the same time protects her against excess energy, so that she will not overreact to sudden events, which in turn could lead to stress.

Allowing a dog to carry something boosts his self-confidence

As mentioned earlier, activity helps to develop the feeling of being in control, that important feeling of being able to deal with various difficulties, instead of feeling powerless and helpless.

Experience has shown that animals that feel they are in control are happier and more active and also have a better immune system.

You can find tips on appropriate training in my book *Mental Training for Your Dog*. Toys that have been designed specifically to stimulate dogs mentally are available to buy from pet shops.

Social confidence is important

Social contact is probably the most important factor in giving a dog security. However, it can also be one of the biggest stress factors. A dog can only feel confident with a confident, quiet owner. In turn, this depends greatly on the owner's level of responsibility, knowledge and character.

The owner must be quiet, reliable and consistent. They should provide their dog with the right amount of physical and mental activity. They should not be aggressive, scream, hit their dog, infantilise, command or constantly control him.

Dogs coexist on the basis of loving benignity, and aggression threatens the cohesion and survival of the pack. Your relationship with your dog should be based on the bond between pack members as much as possible. That means that you should be quiet and friendly and that you and your dog should do a lot together, both physically and mentally.

Shared activities promote development and bonding

Just like a young person, an insecure and stressed dog will develop various behavioural problems early on.

If you punish, discipline, reprimand, fight, are inconsistent and take out your bad moods on your dog then you have to change something about yourself. If you know that you do not do enough with your dog then it is high time you did something about it.

Start right now, because a dog's life is short.

If you have more than one dog, it is important that they get on together, otherwise enormous stress can result. If a similar situation occurred in a wild pack, one member would leave, but dogs in human care have no escape. If a dog does not get on with the other dog(s) she will develop various symptoms of stress fairly quickly.

If you find yourself in a situation like this you should seriously consider giving away one of the dogs, especially the younger one. You may also find that the dog that provokes or is aggressive is ill or in pain, in which case you should talk to a vet. A case of two Cavalier King Charles spaniels is a good example. When dogs of such a peaceful breed become enemies there must be a reason for it, and the reason is usually pain. When the instigator was given medication for pain, the aggression disappeared immediately. Unfortunately I was not able to follow up the case, so I do not know what was wrong with him.

A harmonious pair

The emotional factor

Various types of emotional expression such as empathy or care can counteract stress, stress-related illnesses and negative psychological conditions, both in people and in animals.

As mentioned earlier, the "feel good" hormone oxytocin and pain-relieving endorphins are released when positive physical contact such as cuddling, stroking or massage takes place.

In an experiment, rabbits were fed an unhealthy, high cholesterol diet. Half of them lived in cages and the other half were cared for by staff, taken out of their cages, stroked and given some attention every day. The group that was not cared for developed heart diseases, including hardening of the arteries. Far fewer animals were ill in the group that was given attention. This is called the "emotional factor".

Dogs have many types of behaviour that ensure security and cohesion in the group, so they react particularly sensitively to behaviour that strengthens togetherness. They react even more to behaviour that weakens the pack structure, such as aggression, and this separates pack members, which is similar to what happens when you control and correct your dog.

Physical contact, shared relaxation, games and anything else that has a positive effect on the bond not only improve cohesion but

Stroking releases the "feel good hormone", oxytocin

This dog is motivated and attentive

also prevent stress, stress-related illnesses and a negative psychological state.

It is good to play with your dog, cuddle her, stroke her and give her physical contact, but only as much as your dog wants, because not all dogs like a lot of physical attention. Encouragement, kind words and a gentle voice also help to create harmony, whereas a gruff, demanding and accusatory tone tends to make dogs stressed.

For dogs, the "Rolls Royce" of physical contact is the massage. Treat your dog's muscles to a gentle massage every day. This will enable your dog to deal with negative stress better and more quickly. Take part in one of the many massage and relaxation courses for dog owners, if possible.

Control motivates

Earlier on, I mentioned how important the feeling of control is and that a dog is always somewhere between helplessness, passivity, activity and the feeling of complete control. You can see it as soon as you look at a dog, especially at his eyes. Admittedly, some dogs have an empty or sad look because that is typical for the breed, which means that you then have to look closely at other signs, for example

Agility training can make dogs less sensitive to stress

whether the dog is agile and alert or passive and submissive, whether he takes the initiative or simply waits for your command.

If you let the dog take the initiative or even encourage him to do so, you will improve his feeling of being in control. This feeling will be lost if he is constantly dominated and only has to follow commands.

AGILITY IS GOOD TRAINING

Agility is a sport that involves an obstacle course for dogs. This activity is a wonderful and effective way of helping to develop the feeling of control and, at the same time, of making the dog less sensitive to stress. Of course, the same applies to mental challenges.

Agility improves confidence, especially because the dog learns to control her body and to follow instructions, within seconds, that could lead to major success. When it comes to agility, it does not matter if you train as part of a group or alone with your dog. You can also use any natural obstacles in a park or forest for agility training. Use your imagination. Dog training clubs usually offer agility courses where you can train.

Helplessness – vacant expression ◇ alert expression ◇ mischievous expression ◇ confident expression – Control

Digging can also relieve stress

Your dog can learn to deal with difficulties

In order to foster confidence and the feeling of control, you should teach your dog active strategies that he can apply to a variety of stressful experiences, at least some of the time. Problem solving is based on genetic makeup on the one hand and early experiences on the other. The more serious the situation is, the more difficult it is to solve future problems.

Try to confront puppies with as many demanding or difficult situations as possible. This includes unpleasant contact, examination and treatment at the vet or at the dog groomer's, where young puppies become familiar with pain or being held firmly, approaches by other dogs, gunshot, fireworks and all kinds of disturbances. This all lays the foundation for how dogs deal with problems later in life.

When confronted with threats or other dangerous situations, dogs do not have to choose just between fight and flight. The dog can submit completely, scream in terror, growl, become paralysed by fear, try to dig, and much more. Whatever the dog does, the decision is not based on free will, but on genetics and early experiences.

Psych up your dog by supporting an active but sensible strategy for dealing with difficult situations and teach her to make her first choice something new. Perhaps she will simply find confidence in you. In this case, you will have to guarantee that you will protect your dog and that nothing bad will happen to her. That includes trips to the vet, as well as telling the vet how they should treat the dog, being willing to pay a little more for a longer appointment, declining an examination or asking for a painkiller. The dog will then learn that going to the vet is not so bad after all and will be less stressed.

Predictability

Being able to know and predict what is going to happen gives dogs peace and security. That is why routine is so important for an insecure dog. Keep to a schedule for walks, feeding and other activities.

On the other hand, a balanced dog will find it very boring when everything always runs like clockwork and nothing new or exciting ever happens. Routine is important for insecure dogs that have enough stress already and find life difficult. However, even insecure dogs will benefit when something unusual happens occasionally, if it is fun or interesting. Enjoyable, unusual activities such as a longer walk or tracking work do not put dogs under strain.

The social environment has to be consistent in order for it to be predictable for a dog. Always treat the dog the same way. What is allowed; what is not allowed – no exceptions. What is forbidden is always forbidden. Dogs feel secure when they know the rules.

However, following the rules should not be enforced with strict commands and punishment, but with consistency and respect for the dog. If he jumps up on the sofa (if this is not allowed), quietly coax him down and praise him when he lies on the floor. You do not need to do anything else.

Control of other hormones

It is not unusual for dogs to have too much or too little of certain hormones. Because the hormone system works as a unit, excessive or insufficient production of individual hormones can influence the others and lead to an imbalance in the system as a whole. The hormone thyroxine, produced by the thyroid gland, seems to be particularly sensitive, as does the male hormone testosterone.

Vets investigate the thyroid by doing a blood test. Testosterone levels are usually not tested, but we can assume that a male dog who produces too much testosterone (or with increased sensitivity to this hormone) will develop enhanced masculine characteristics. These include raised stress levels, a particular interest in urine scents and female dogs, a tendency to scrap with other male dogs and a very small appetite (although this does not affect most retriever and some spaniel breeds).

Illness and pain as a cause

Pain and illness are major stress factors that can affect animals in two main ways. The pain itself and the other symptoms of an illness are the primary reason for stress. It hurts! Furthermore, pain and illness restrict movement and other behaviour patterns.

Dogs need to be mentally and physically challenged

Although many people would deny it, illness and pain are often the cause of stress. The sufferer quickly finds out how to soothe the pain. Movement, being alert to anything interesting and being on edge are typical behaviours that

soothe pain or get rid of unpleasant feelings in the short term. This applies to people and to other animals, especially dogs.

Some dogs cannot rest, especially when they are outside, but also indoors. They whine and run around for no apparent reason and appear restless and stressed. Their behaviour is perhaps an attempt to relieve pain.

Dogs that are obsessed with certain things or ways of behaving, such as being on the lookout for cats or other dogs, playing fetching games with people or eating small stones are typical examples of animals with compulsive behaviour.

Dogs may be more stressed than the situation in question warrants, overreact with exuberance when they go out, or attack other dogs even if there is no reason for aggression. These are other examples of how behaviour can soothe pain.

Of course there could be other reasons for this behaviour, but you should consider the possibility of illness and pain. If you find out that the dog is in pain, for example because of toothache, headache or muscular pain, it is relatively easy to alleviate the cause of the stress.

Concentrating on the job in hand

Make your dog work mentally – she should use the part of her brain that is responsible for concentration, evaluation, calculation, comparison and other things on which a dog needs to concentrate. These processes take place mainly in the frontal lobes. With training, cognitive functions will improve control of the limbic system and the areas of the brain that control feelings.

Games of skill like this stimulate brain activity

These processes are part of activating the mind, which helps the dog to learn to follow a trail, to balance and to solve problems. These activities require focus, concentration, assessment and evaluation and are the best training for the brain, so that the dog learns to get her emotions under control.

Get your dog to perform "brain" tasks as often as possible. Variety is important so if you give your dog a little task, make sure that it is bigger the next time. Tailor it to your day-to-day life by doing more when you have a lot of time and less when you don't.

Do not feel guilty! It is OK if you sometimes cut down on activities like this in our fast-moving times. Even wild dogs are more active at some times and less active at others. If a wolf pack kills an elk, the pack will have a few days of relaxa-tion during which they just eat, sleep and per-haps work a little to protect the prey from crows or other animals.

You can also choose activities that do not take up much time, for example scattering treats in the garden or wrapping them up so that the dog has to unwrap them. These exercises do not take long, but they get the dog's attention for a certain time.

When you go for a walk, take the opportunity to stop every now and then at certain "stations" en route where you can ask your dog to perform mental activities. They can be as simple as look-ing for a dropped glove or key, balancing on a wall or fallen tree, getting round an obstacle to get to a treat or learning new tasks or tricks. There are lots of different options if you are creative or look for ideas in books.

Environmental stimuli

To make a dog more resilient, he should first get used to everything that happens in his environment and also to things that do not happen very often, such as gunshots, thunder and fireworks. The stimuli that cause the most stress and trauma to dogs are loud and sudden noises. Play your dog a CD with sounds of gunshot, thunder and fireworks.

It is always best to confront a dog with different sounds and experiences when he is still a puppy. However, most dogs are older when they experience their first shock or are exposed to long-term stress. You can get an older dog used to these stimuli using the methods described above, but the sessions should be longer and more frequent.

Situations that require direct physical contact, such as a trip to the dog groomer or vet, must also be practised frequently, because these experiences are unnatural and compromise the dog's integrity. Dogs will often defend themselves against people who force them to do things such as opening their mouth, sticking things in their ears, clipping their nails or laying them on their side to examine them.

If you get a dog used to standing still on a table or on the floor for various examinations, you can "immunise" him so that he feels less uncomfortable in these unpleasant situations. It is important that you practise this often, but each session should not last too long and should always end with a reward. Ask your vet (and somebody from the dog groomer's if your dog has to go there) whether you can bring your dog for a trial visit before he is actually treated for the first time.

Control and the feeling of being in control

The knowledge that you can control a situation is important for counteracting negative stress. We can give our dogs that knowledge quite easily.

By preparing a dog for what is happening, we can reinforce her feeling that she has the situation under control. Naturally this is not always possible, but it can be enough to make sure, as often as possible, that the dog is not surprised by new experiences. How you get your dog used to new experiences depends on the individual and the situation. You can achieve a lot just by naming the terms that your dog associates with other dogs, people and events.

"We're going to the park."

"Fred's coming over."

"Wait here. I'll be right back."

"We're going to the vet."

The more a dog associates with the words and the more she knows their meaning, the better she can prepare herself for pleasant and unpleasant experiences. She will feel that she has everything under control if she knows what will happen before the actual situation takes place.

When the dog is confronted with a new situation, she will need a routine that she can follow. For example, when you arrive at the park or another place that you often visit, you should devise a certain sequence that you and your dog consistently follow. Start with a special walk in which you incorporate exercises that your dog knows well. Stay with your dog the entire time. If you have to leave her alone anywhere, in the car for example, try to make sure that you are

Dogs listen, so you should always talk to them to prepare them for what is going to happen

always away for the same length of time (as short as possible).

In every new place, allow your dog a "habituation period" of around 10 to 20 minutes. If it is somewhere with other dogs, such as a dog show, training club or even a park, your dog will notice that she has entered other dogs' territory. Your dog will behave as if she has entered an unknown territory and will become insecure and submissive. This place is not her home, it smells of other dogs and there are also other dogs present, which is a not good environment for training or for achieving goals.

During the "habituation period", let your dog investigate everything, sniff, attend to her business and explore the area and other people and dogs. Physical exercise will warm up her muscles and she will have, just like her owner, enough time to prepare mentally for the next step.

We usually have special clothes for different activities. When you put on your coat and pick up certain things to go for a walk, such as a lead, the dog gets information about what is going to happen next. Make sure that you are consistent about the clothes and equipment you use

Dogs at a dog show need some time to settle down

for doing certain things. You should not put on your walking jacket and then leave your dog at home by herself. When possible, wear different clothes for walking and for activities in which your dog is not involved.

Fear of thunder

When dogs are afraid of thunder, it is often not just the sound that frightens them. In his book *The Dog who Loved Too Much*, Nicolas Dodman writes that the fear may have something to do with static charge. He established that many dogs seek protection in the bathroom, in damp cellars or in the garage during storms. The piping and moisture in these rooms earth the surroundings and drain away the tension.

That means that when a storm comes, you can earth your dog with a damp cloth and contact with a metal object. If he is very anxious you can also protect his ears with cotton wool and give him a mild sedative. As long as your dog does not panic, herbal remedies are usually sufficient.

How you can heal your dog

Problem behaviour always creates stress, just as if the dog is afraid of something or wants to attack something. Anxiety, hyperactivity, constant whining or barking are also signs of stress. The most common advice given to dog owners is to punish the symptoms. The reasons given for these symptoms are generally incorrect leadership by the owner or that the dog is spoilt.

Forget it! Punishing a dog for showing problem behaviour is totally wrong and is based on old-school theories that no longer stand up in the face of modern knowledge. Furthermore, punishment is unethical and wholly unnecessary when there are so many modern and effective methods for helping dogs. To solve the problem, you should look for the actual cause instead of working on training methods. The dog may be understimulated or in pain, her hormones could be out of balance, there could be a lack of serotonin activity in her brain. Those are just some of the possible causes.

If you have found and closely analysed the real reason, the next step is simple: the dog will recover quickly when you work on remedying the cause.

The dog will then not need to be trained because she will find her balance by herself. However, sometimes she will need a little training and this should always be gentle and positive. Clicker training is very promising and often used for dogs with problems.

Training based on punishing the symptoms is only effective for a short time. If you consider the reasons for the problem behaviour, the end result will last, the training will not be unpleasant for the dog, and you and your dog will enjoy a better relationship together.

References

APDT Newsletter March/April, 2002.

Arborelius, L.
Mentalitet och Personlighet hos Hunden.
(The mentality and personality of the dog –
article) Artikel i Shiban, medlemsblad för
Shiba-no-kai. Nr. 4/2008
.

Beazley, M.
Forums Stora boken om människan
(The Great Book about Human Beings).
Bokförlaget Forum, Stockholm, Sweden, 1978.

Bra Böckers Stora läkarlexikon
(Swedish Publisher Bra Böckers' Great
Medical Dictionary), 1992.

CD – Fyrverkeri, åska och skott.
Ljud för hundträning
(Fireworks, thunder and shots.
Audio CD for dog training).
Jycke-Tryck AB, Sweden.

Christianson, S.-Å.
Traumatiska minnen Natur och Kultur
(Traumatic Memories).
Stockholm, Sweden, 2002.

Cloninger, R., Masters, R. & McGuire, M.
(Editors).
The Neurotransmitter Revolution. Southern
Illinois University Press, Carbondale, IL, 1994.

Dodman, N.
The Dog who Loved Too Much.
Bantam, 1996.

Fogle, B.
I huvudet på en hund (Inside a Dog's Head).
Bokförlaget Forum, Sweden, 1991.

Fox, M.
Understanding your Dog.
Coward, McCann & Geoghegan, Inc.,
New York, 1972.

Frankenhaeuser, M. & Ödman, M.
Stress, en del av livet (Stress – Part of Life).
Brombergs Bokförlag AB, Värnamo,
Sweden, 1983.

Hallgren, A.
Tikens dominans. Undersökningsrapport
(Bitch Dominance, Investigative Report).
Jycke-Tryck, Vagnhärad, Sweden, 1988.

Hallgren, A.
Alfa Syndromet – om ledarskap och rangordning
hos hundar (The Alpha Syndrome – about dog
leadership and rank).
ICA Bokförlag, Västerås, Sweden, 2006.

Hallgren, A.
Mental Activation.
Cadmos, Schwarzenbek, 2007.

Hallgren, A.
Problemhund och hund problem
(Problem Dog and Dog Problems).
ICA Bokförlag, Västerås, Sweden, 1971/2008.

Hallgren, A. Back Problems in Dogs –
a research study (1994).
Dogma, Stockholm, 2010

Hansson, M.
Min Bästa Vän – aktivering och dogpsykologi
(My Best Friend – activation and dog
psychology).
Jycke-Tryck AB, Falkenberg, 1984/2007

Hansson, M.
Kan auktoritär uppfostran öka risken för
hundaggression? Pilotstudie, opublicerad (Can
an authoritarian upbringing bring on increased
aggression in dogs? Unpublished Pilot Study),
1994.

Harlow, H. F.
The nature of love.
American Psychologist, 1958, 13, 673–685.

Hart, B. & Hart, L.
Canine and Feline Behavioral Therapy.
Lea & Febiger,
Philadelphia, 1985.

Haug, L.
Impulsivity and behavioral disorders. Part I + II.
APDT Newsletter May/June + July/August 2007.

Jensen, P.
Prenatal stress.
Adventure Dog Conference,
Södertälje, Sweden, 2004.

Kylling, R.
Stoffskifteforstyrrelser og atferdsendringer hos
hunden
(Hormonal Changes and Behavioural Problems
in Dogs), Stencil, 2004.

Lane, J. Stress and cortisol.
Lecture for Svenska Service – och Signalhunds-
förbundets konferens i Malmö,
Sweden, October 2006.

Løberg, G. Valpesocialisering
(Socializing the Puppy).
Canis AS, Melhus, Norge, 2007.

Magnusson, E.
Parental investment hos tamhund
(Parental investment in the Domesticated Dog).
D/E-arbete. Institute of Zoology,
Stockholm University, 1981.

Malm, K.
Människan, Relationen Hunden
(Man, Relationships, Dog).
K. MalmTanke i Tryck,
Skara, Sweden, 2005.

Masters, R. & McGuire, M. (Editors).
The Neurotransmitter Revolution.
Southern Illinois University Press,
Carbondale, IL, 1994.

Morris, D. & Lithgow, S.
Training and Working Dogs –
for quiet confident control of stock.
University of Queensland Press, 1991

Nagel, M. & von Reinhardt, C.
Stressade Hundar (Stressed Dogs).
ICA Bokförlag, Sweden, 2005.

O'Heare, J.
Canine neuropsychology and dog training.
APDT Newsletter March/April 2002.

Peterson, K., Prout, M. & Schwarz, A.
Post-Traumatic Stress Disorder,
A Clinician's Guide.
Plenum Press, New York and London, 1991.

Rugaas, T.
Personlig kommunikation
(Personal communication), 2009.

Schilder, M., & van der Borg, J.
Training dogs with help of the shock collar;
short and long term behavioural effects.
Applied Animal Behavior Science,
2004, 85, 319–334.

Scott, J. P. & Fuller, J.
Genetics and the Social Behavior of the Dog.
The University of Chicago Press, 1965.

Seligman, M.
Hjälplöshet (Helplessness).
Aldus/Bonniers, Stockholm, 1976.

Selin, D.
Personlig kommunikation
(Personal communication).
1993–2009.

Zimen, E.
The Wolf – a Species in Danger.
Delacorte Press, New York, 1981.

Index

CADMOS
Dog Guides

Angie Mienk

The Invisible Link to Your Dog

Times when dogs were trained to be only obedient or to carry out certain tasks are long gone. Many dog owners today wish to have a relationship based on mutual understanding and a much closer bond to their four-legged friend. This book presents a unique method that will help readers develop non-verbal, almost intuitive communication with their dogs.

80 pages, Paperback
ISBN 978-0-85788-201-1

Kerstin Mielke

Anatomy of the Dog

Many dog owners are fascinated not only by the colouring and character of their dog, but also by their physique and harmonious movements. If you want to find out more about the inner organs, skin and coat, nervous system and senses join a fascinating journey through your dog´s body.

96 pages, Paperback
ISBN 978-3-86127-979-2

Uli Köppel

The Pack Concept

The author has developed a completely new approach: relationship training for the human-dog-team, in place of exploitive training. Humans and dogs have been cohabiting closely for millennia. To help us understanding this special relationship, and above all, in order to make it a successful one, Uli Köppel has developed the species-appropriate concept of pack behaviour.

128 pages, Paperback
ISBN 978-3-86127-958-7

Martina Nau

Snooping around!

This book contains a wealth of ideas on how everybody can keep their dogs busy and entertained with games all around their sense of smell. The tasks and games described here will entertain both the human and their dog, challenging and employing a dog's instincts, and will ultimately strengthen the relationship between us and our dog companions.

80 pages, Paperback
ISBN 978-0-85788-200-4

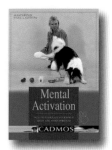

Anders Hallgren

Mental Activation

Every dog needs encounter, and overcome, physical and mental challenges, for the sake of its basic well-being. The author describes simple exercises designed to stimulate and improve your dog´ senses. It is not vital that the dog learns to perform these tasks perfectly, for the main aim is to challenge its mind and intelligence.

96 pages, Paperback
ISBN 978-3-86127-927-3

For more information, please visit:
www.cadmos.co.uk

CADMOS